Understanding the Cat

In Taoism, a master is not someone who dominates other creatures or other objects. A master is someone who understands the innate nature of a thing so well that he becomes a part of it. For example, a master boatman knows the water so well that he flows with it.

To have a loving, meaningful relationship with our cats, we need to understand and appreciate the innate nature of our animal companions.

When we understand the innate nature of our animal companions, we can provide them with the environment that appeals to that nature. We can help them be stimulated, satisfied, and content.

Books by Deborah Wood

The Tao of Bow Wow
The Tao of Meow

The Tao of Meow

UNDERSTANDING AND TRAINING YOUR CAT THE TAOIST WAY

DEBORAH WOOD

A DELL TRADE PAPERBACK

A DELL TRADE PAPERBACK

Published by
Dell Publishing
a division of
Random House, Inc.
New York, New York

The trademark Dell® is registered in the U.S. Patent and
Trademark Office.

Library of Congress Cataloging in Publication Data

Wood, Deborah, 1952
The Tao of meow meow : understanding and training your
cat the taoist way / Deborah Wood.
p.   cm.
Includes bibliographical references.
ISBN 978-0-440-50867-0
1. Cats — Behavior.   2. Cats — Training.   3. Taoism.
4. Human-animal communication.   I. Title.
SF446.5.W66   1999
636.8 — dc21   99-13630
CIP

Book design by Julie Duquet

Published simultaneously in Canada

*To the four-footed sages who have
changed my life*

Acknowledgments

There would be no *The Tao of Meow* without Charles Wu's encouragement, gentle correction, and sense of humor. What other Chinese scholar could help me find the Taoist principle that applies to helping a cat use his scratching post?

Tommie Brunick, after twenty-five years of caring for homeless, unwanted animals, still sees the spirit in every creature who walks across her path. She has taught me volumes about how to make an animal's shattered life whole again.

Many other people have helped me gain insights into Taoist thought and into the ways of the cat. Thank you, Robert Anderson, D.V.M., Leah Atwood, Professor Chen Hui-Xian, Jeff Judkins, D.V.M., Li Pingping, Janie Lineberry, Roger Lore, Mary Mandeville, D.C., Sarahjoy Marsh, Myrla Magness, Susan Mentley, Cindy Miller, Betty Namie, Lynn Potter, Chip Sammons, and Arlette Sieckman, N.D., L.Ac. Your wisdom helped these pages come to life.

Jim Hornfischer of The Literary Group International is a literary agent who fully appreciates the spirit of my books. Diane Bartoli has a gentle spirit and warmth that are rare gifts in an editor. Thank you both for helping me translate my ideas into your world.

I deeply appreciate the cats in my life who have taught me. Special love to Silver Lining and Mews, who have so clearly shown me their own soft lights.

Contents

Foreword

I believe that truth with a capital "T" must hold
true within all levels of experience: physical/
biological, emotional, spiritual. Always I ask myself, "Can I see this Truth revealed in Nature? Is
it as real in the interaction between my dog and
cat as it is between me and my human family?
Can I carry this Truth to the heavens with me?"
If the answer to any one of these questions is no,
then I am not seeing Truth. I also believe that if
ancient Truths are indeed true, they should be
applicable to all generations, for all times.

Taoism is Truth. Its admonition to acknowledge the strength of stillness and of one's innate
nature, to nurture the healing flow of energy
among one another, and to follow the soul path
of least resistance is remarkably sound advice
for those of us living in this astonishing, con-
founding, treacherous, and exhilarating twenty-
first century. Clearly, the Way of the Tao is as

relevant today as in centuries past when it was first put into words.

The gift that Deborah Wood brings to our understanding of the Tao with her new book *The Tao of Meow*, is a wonderfully fresh concept of how this ancient teaching applies to our daily lives with our feline companions. I never cease to be amazed and delighted when someone uses ancient Truth in an entirely new way, and Deborah has done exactly that.

There have been few seasons in my adult life when I have not kept company with cats. Although I call myself a dog person by nature — animated, extroverted, approval-seeking — I seem to require the balancing energy of cats in my life. In their stillness and grace, in their need for solitary space and "meditation" time, I am reminded of my deep and healing need for these elements in my own life.

Currently, two cats share my home. Flora is a ten-year-old tuxedo cat, and a survivor of feline leukemia. Mirella, my young gray tabby, is of feral origin and was converted to a house cat because of my needs, not hers. Left to her own preferences, she would be languishing in bales of sweet green hay, reigning as the Queen of the Barn. Different in character as winter and summer, these two cats work hard to keep me on the path of the Tao.

Stillness. It is mid-morning and I am in my basement office sorting and reading mail, answering e-mail messages, filing letters, returning phone calls, stacking book boxes, and looking under stacks of paper for my lost coffee cup. As is my nature, I am doing all these things at once. Flora flounces down the stairs, tail skyward, muttering to me as she comes. She has always been a chatty cat, speaking in long sentences consisting of various forms of "Waah." As usual, her voice is cranky and nagging. "Waaah wa WAAAAwa wah . . ." she admonishes as she marches toward my legs. The instant I sit down to fiddle through a desk drawer, she springs onto my lap. She stomps, circles, complains, then settles down with a heavy plop. There. She has me. Flora knows I am not one to toss a comfortable cat off my lap easily. My frantic scrambling throughout the office ceases suddenly as Flora claims me for the moment. In the small circle of motion her presence allows me, I can reach only a few files, my computer, and the phone. "Well," I say to myself, "best start here." Flora begins to purr and make paddy-paws on my leg. My fussiness melts into some semblance of focus. As annoyed as I am in having to remain pinned to my seat and work around my cat, I realize that Flora is bringing me an enforced moment of stillness, and I grudgingly thank her for her efforts.

Innate Nature. Each winter little Mirella becomes an indoor cat. Our snows here in the Rocky Mountain West are high, and temperatures are bitterly low. When the ground goes pillowy white in November, I stop opening the door for Mirella's daily forays into the pasture. Within days she gives up her vigil by the back door and adjusts herself to six months of indoor living. Mirella was born in a barn of a wild mother. Although she has blossomed into the most affectionate cat I have ever been blessed to know, she retains much of her farm-girl nature. Her pasture hunts in winter become stalking games on the carpet, where she chases shadows and sunbeams. She lurks in hidden corners so that she can spring out and smack the dogs as they wander innocently past. Stacks of hay are replaced by solitary haunts high on our tallest pieces of furniture. No insect is safe. Afternoon naps in the barn loft become lazy snoozes on the sun-drenched windowsills. Somehow her soul follows her into the house and finds expression there. Her balance awes me. That she can be who she is no matter the circumstance is a lesson in the Tao that I have yet to achieve. I, too, am at heart a wild farm girl, yet without a barn to romp in, my soul's expression constricts into distraction and anxiety. Far better to learn to nap on windowsills and stalk bugs—to keep the soul of the farm deep inside—as Mirella so gently reminds me.

The path of least resistance. I seemed to have absorbed the idea from the very air that hard work and struggle are the tools of success. If something comes easily, it can't be worth much. Because I am a slow learner, it has taken me almost fifty years of living to prove myself wrong in this belief. My cats have helped me along the way. Never-never-never do I see Flora or Mirella throw themselves forcefully against any challenge. When I shut the door on Mirella in the winter, she makes her way to every other window and door in the house to see if there is another way out. Finally, she will return to sit quietly at the closed door, taking a few days to peacefully reinvent herself as an indoor cat. Since she's made herself offensive to the dogs by bopping them unmercifully at every opportunity, Mirella has had to find a way of living indoors with two very large and mistrustful canine companions. To move through the house without being growled at, she simply takes wide detours around both dogs. If they are blocking her way, she finds another way to get to where she wants to go—perhaps over the furniture, or under a table and around the chairs. She never gives up on her final destination, and she never argues with anyone over how to get there. She flows.

Although Mirella is a diligent and patient hunter of window-buzzing flies, Flora is a more advanced student of the Tao in this arena. Flora waits until the flies drop dead, then carries them off for a snack. She must have read *The Book of Chuang Tzu*, which states: "One who follows the Tao daily does less and less. As he does less and less, he eventually arrives at actionless action. Having achieved actionless action, there is nothing which is not done." That's Flora. Nonaction at its finest.

The Tao of Meow also contains useful sections on the Tao of cat training. I must admit that I always thought that cat training meant the cat's methods for training his or her human companion. At least that's how this always works at my house. My cats have always been flawlessly effective at training me. They wait by the food bowl. I fill it. They wait by the litter box. I clean it. They wait by my side. I invite them into my

lap. Both of my cats have Taoist nonaction training techniques down to a science. It is a novel
idea to me that I could perhaps apply these con-
cepts to my cats and train them. I may give this
a try. I truly doubt that I will have as good success with my cats as they have had with me.
They are far better teachers than I.

These and many more cat-inspired insights
have come to me since reading Deborah Wood's
wonderful book, *The Tao of Meow.* I have had a
copy of the *Tao Te Ching* at home for years, yet
never fully appreciated just how masterful my
animal companions are in applying its tenets. To
apply ancient Truth to present-day challenges is
the mark of a wise teacher, and I feel Deborah
Wood has answered such a calling in her writing. As people who love animals—and you must
be one, too, or you wouldn't be holding this
book—we must constantly seek kinder and
more respectful ways of living with them. Applying the wisdom of the Tao, as Deborah Wood
suggests, is a wonderful and innovative way to

achieve a healthier relationship with the cats —
or with any animals — who share our home.

Susan Chernak McElroy
Animals As Teachers and Healers
Animals As Guides for the Soul
7505 North Roberta Drive
Jackson, WY 83001
(307)734-7107
smcelroy@wyoming.com

PART ONE

Lessons from the Tao

I

The Tao of the Cat

My small friend sitting on the windowsill understands the primal, natural ways of the world. She leaps into the air, ethereal as sunlight, and connects to the energy of the sky. She relaxes her body so profoundly that she becomes heavy to lift, rooted to the energy of the earth. She is loving yet independent, wiry yet soft, ferocious yet friendly.

A cat is the ultimate Taoist.

Put simply, Taoism (pronounced Dow-ism) is a philosophy that believes there is a universal energy to the world. The Tao (pronounced Dow) is the energy that encompasses, permeates, and governs the entire universe. This energy flows through all living creatures. If we block this flow of energy, we suffer from physical, emotional, and spiritual malaise. Taoism is a philosophy that can be compatible with most religions and spiritual beliefs. Many Christians and Buddhists are also Taoists.

It is impossible to explain Taoism in a paragraph—or in a million words. Lao Tzu, the philosophy's most revered sage, admonished more than two thousand years ago:

> The Tao that can be told
>   is not the eternal Tao.
> The name that can be named
>   is not the eternal name.[1]

In fact, reading the pale shadow of meaning that words can convey is the source of some amusement to people who are deeply connected to this powerful philosophy. The best way to learn about Taoism is to experience it and to live it—and to study with a teacher who understands its ways. Cats are exceptional teachers and can help us to find the healthy, healing light of the Tao.

The precepts of Taoism, with their focus on natural balance, healthy life, and gentle respect for all creatures, can help us become better friends and guardians of our cats. Learning from our animal companions and then using that knowledge to help our fellow creatures: That's a perfect example of living in the Tao.

2

THE EQUALITY OF ALL THINGS: LESSONS FROM THE CAT

Lao Tzu wrote:

Anyone who doesn't respect a teacher
or cherish a student
may be clever, but has gone astray.[1]

Cats as Teachers

Westerners usually dismiss the possibility of learning profound life lessons from a "pet." Our philosophical tradition dictates that we are of a higher level of being than the animals around us.

We train animals, we house them, we may even love them, but we never think of them as being our peers.

Taoist tradition is very different. According to Taoism, all things are a part of the universal energy flow. Therefore, all things are equal. A king is not better than a pauper. An adult is not better than a child. A human is not better than a cat.

The Book of Chuang Tzu, one of the basic writings of Taoism, tells us, "To have a human form is a joyful thing. But in the universe of possible forms, there are others just as good."[2]

When Chen Fuyin, a Chinese master of qigong (a form of meditative exercise), visited Oregon, I went to hear him speak since I practice qigong. He told the following story about the Taoist principle of equality:

An archer was shooting in the woods when he lost an arrow. He was an enlightened man and said to himself, "It does not matter that I have lost my arrow, because whoever finds the arrow will be a person from my province. Because we both come from the same province, it is just the same for the other man to have the arrow as it is for me to have it."

Later, the archer told this story to Confucius. "You are right as far as you went," said Confucius, "but it doesn't matter what province the man who finds the arrow comes from. You are both humans, and it is just the same for any other human to have the arrow as it is for you to have it."

The sage Lao Tzu heard the story and corrected Confucius. "You are right as far as you went, too," Lao Tzu told Confucius. "But it doesn't matter if the arrow was found by a man or by another creature. We are all creatures, and it is just the same for any animal to have the arrow as it is for the archer to have it."

Your relationship with your animal companion will be transformed when you adopt the Taoist perspective of animals as our equals. This viewpoint requires you to respect and honor your cat. It underlines the preciousness of her health and her very being.

When our human friends grow and develop from the events that happen in their lives, we learn those lessons with them. When we have a human friend with an extraordinary skill, we are pleased and proud when that friend teaches us her craft. If we consider our animal companions to be our equals, we can learn life lessons from them in a similar fashion.

In the Taoist view of the world, teachers aren't necessarily human. So open your heart to what your cat can teach you. You may be in for some delightful surprises.

3

YIN AND YANG:
PERFECT BALANCE

*Perfect yin is harsh and cold, perfect yang is
awesome and fiery. Harshness and coldness
emanate from Earth, awesomeness and
fieriness emanate from Heaven. The two mingle
and join, and from their conjunction comes to
birth everything that lives.[1]*

The yin-yang symbol (also called the map of
the Great Ultimate) is a circle, half filled with an
arc of white, half with an arc of dark. This symbol epitomizes the Taoist reverence for balance.
The light (yang) and dark (yin) are perfectly
counterbalanced and intertwined. Yang is the
energy from heaven—and all things light, hot,
and male. Yin is the energy from earth—and all
things dark, cool, and female. Life occurs when
yin and yang come together and interact. The
ideal existence would have a perfect balance between yin and yang.

The symbol for Taoism could just as well have

been a cat. No creature on this planet is more perfectly balanced. It is the balance of yin and yang, sleep and action, relaxation and focus, tame and wild, that defines the lives of our cats.

A cat has extraordinary yang energy. He hangs in the air, suspended, as he pounces. He races up a tree faster than the animals who live in the branches. With ease and grace, a cat can leap up onto surfaces five times his height. He hunts his prey with wondrous intensity. A cat epitomizes the fire and strength of energy from the heavens.

Cats have equally remarkable yin energy. When a cat rests, his body is so relaxed that he seems to melt into the cushion. He has turned sleeping into an art form. His coat is soft and gentle to touch. He is quiet. A cat demonstrates the calm, patient silence of energy from the earth.

In the yin-yang symbol, the line that divides yin from yang is not a straight one. It is curved, like a resting cat's back. There is always a light spot of yang in the arc of yin, and a dark spot of yin in the light of yang. A cat demonstrates this constant flow and interaction between yin and yang in countless ways. For example, the hard muscles of a cat's body are clothed in plush fur. Fierce talons are sheathed by round, soft paws.

From our cats we can learn to have a better, healthier balance between yin and yang. If we allow them, they can teach us this harmony.

Physical Balance

The cat is perhaps this world's most perfectly physically balanced creature. Nature built the cat with strong muscles, ideally suited for leaping and climbing. His shoulders and chest are constructed differently from other mammals', allowing him more flexibility of movement.

But the cat's equilibrium is more than just his structure. You can see your cat use the energy from the earth and the energy from the sky in every motion he makes.

The cat's most startling demonstration of his balance between heaven and earth is his ability to fall from heights and almost always land safely on his feet. Scientists have studied this unique ability. Research has demonstrated that a falling cat first twists his head to be level with the ground. Once his head is oriented correctly between heaven and earth, the cat usually is able to move his body around and land on all four paws.

Practitioners of moving meditation forms such as yoga, tai chi, and qigong know the magic of the cat's ability to land on all four feet. At the top of our heads is an acupoint called bai hui (pronounced by-whey). Energy from throughout the universe converges and flows into our bodies through bai hui. It is the balance point for all movement.

By leveling his head first, the cat puts bai hui in its correct position between heaven and earth. He can then line up the rest of his body in relationship to bai hui. As a result, the cat is naturally balanced even as he is falling.

Your cat uses this acupoint to balance himself in every situation, not just in falls. He holds his head level and steady as he walks, runs, or jumps. His head may be high to signal to you that it is mealtime. He may keep his head low in a hunting crouch. Whether your cat's head is held high or low, it is always level, with bai hui at the top of his body's outline.

You can sense the flow of energy from bai hui at the top of your cat's head, down his spine, and through his legs. His posture allows qi (energy) to flow into his head and through his body, ensuring that he is always physically oriented between the earth and sky.

Lesson from the Cat: Improving Balance

Cats are born with the knowledge of bai hui. People have to learn it.

Look straight ahead, eyes level with the horizon. Touch the part of your head that is the highest. (It will be about an inch in front of the back of your skull.) This is bai hui. When you touch bai hui, it will be a little more sensitive than the rest of the top of your head.

Bai hui allows qi to flow into your body.

When you hold your head level so that bai hui is closest to heaven, your qi will flow correctly and you will have excellent balance.

People who learn moving meditation forms such as yoga, tai chi, and qigong are taught to imagine that their bodies are suspended from a golden heavenly string attached to bai hui. (Dance instructors who know nothing about these forms of meditation have long told their students to imagine that their heads are held up by a string.) Try walking across the room with your head level, with bai hui at the uppermost point of your head, suspended by the heavenly string. Now try walking with your head tilted down or to the side: You will feel the difference in your balance.

Observe your cat when he gets up from a nap. He holds his head level as he unfolds himself. Next time you want to get up off the floor, hold your head level with bai hui hung by a heavenly string, focus your eyes on the horizon, and get up. Rising in this way is incomparably easier than if you try to get up while focusing your eyes on the floor.

Cats know the secret of bai hui. If you follow your cat's example, you will begin to develop some of his grace and balance.

As you strive for this balance, the perfection of your cat's physical grace becomes even more striking. We humans can never fully equal the cat's ability to mix yin and yang, heaven and earth, action and stillness. We can only admire this creature who has reached the Taoist ideal of perfect physical harmony.

The Tail

A cat's harmony with earth and sky is not limited to his relationship with bai hui. In fact, nowhere is the cat's perfect balance of yin and yang more apparent than in his tail. Your cat's tail balances the qi in his body. When a cat is feeling social and outgoing—yang behaviors— he pokes his tail straight into the air, absorbing yang energy. When your cat is walking across the room and wants his privacy, his tail droops toward the ground, absorbing the quiet yin energy of the earth.

Your cat's tail balances his body. The tail also enhances his balance by absorbing energy from the earth or sky to suit the cat's purpose.

Watch your cat when he is about to pounce. He roots himself firmly in the ground, absorbing energy from the earth. But the tip of his tail curves to the sky to absorb yang energy. As the tail absorbs more and more fiery yang energy, it twitches. Soon it is twitching so much that your cat's back legs are moving in rhythm with his tail. Finally, his powerful back legs, full of awesome yang energy, leap heavenward as your cat pounces.

Social Balance

Book after book claims that cats are asocial creatures who are aloof and prefer to be alone. Nothing could be further from the truth.

Our feline companions, to varying degrees according to their personalities and life experiences, enjoy their friendships with people, other cats, and other creatures. Cats would not be the most popular animal companion in America if they were asocial and aloof.

Many cats enjoy multiple-cat households where the animals groom each other, sleep intertwined, and play with each other. Countless cats have become inseparable friends with dogs, horses, rabbits, and other animals.

At least once a day my cat, Mews, pounces on my two dogs and initiates a raucous game of tag. My animal companions race through the house, repeatedly changing roles of predator and prey among the three of them. When the game is over, they share the water dish and flop down next to each other, content and relaxed.

Of course, cats aren't always social.

Cats have a natural balance between the need to be social and the need to be alone. Every cat must spend uninterrupted time by himself every day. He may choose to spend his alone time grooming himself, sleeping, or staring out the window. Whatever he does during this time, he makes it clear that no intrusions are welcome.

Our cats enjoy company but also recognize the importance of time spent in seclusion. While they absorb energy from their human and animal companions, they also absorb energy from their solitude.

4

Qi: Vital Life Force

When yin and yang mix, qi is created. Qi (pronounced chee) is the tangible energy that pervades every being. When we are healthy, qi is flowing within our bodies. The energy flows from our hearts, to our spleens, to our lungs, to our kidneys, to our livers, and back to our hearts. This internal flow of energy is important to our physical and mental health. If qi is blocked in any location, we become sick.

In addition to the energy flow within our bod-

ies, we need to experience a flow of energy between our bodies and the universe around us.
Just as we inhale and exhale air, we absorb and
exude qi. It is the flow of qi that makes us
healthy, vital, creative, and connected to the
Tao.

Cat's Paws

Although we absorb qi through our skin, certain
acupoints exchange qi with the universe in a
more concentrated fashion. One of those acupoints is bai hui, at the top of our heads. Four
other key acupoints for people are in the palms
of our hands and just behind the balls of our
feet.

The most sensitive part of a cat's body is the
bottom of her four feet. No matter how rough
the terrain or how many miles a cat travels, her
pads are always soft to the touch. This would
seem to be a foolish design for a cat, since a
hunter would benefit from tough pads.

However, it only makes sense for Nature to

design the cat with naked feet so that she can absorb earth energy through these key acupoints. In fact, because cats are such creatures of the air, the energy flow from their feet to the ground is especially important—it provides an anchor.

Mostly, cats almost float on their feet. But sometimes, cats stomp. A stomping cat can shake the floorboards in an old house. Feet fall heavily to the floor, declaring that this place is the cat's territory, the cat's home. One can almost see the flow of energy between the cat's feet and the earth when a cat stomps.

The Internal Arts

Cats are the world's most accomplished meditators. It is through the stillness of meditation that the exchange of qi is at its most effective. Although the body is still, there is great motion going on inside, as qi flows through the internal organs. This is the Taoist state of motion within the stillness.

Daily hours of meditation can account for our cats' seeming mysteriousness. When people meditate regularly, they experience a rich inner life and are tuned in to the sense of mystery of the universe. Cats, who seem as internally attuned as they are externally attuned, undoubtedly receive the same benefits from meditation that humans do.

Stationary Meditation

Meditation is a fundamental practice of Taoism. By sitting perfectly still we can feel the energy of the earth and the sky. We experience our oneness with nature. Although it is not necessary to sit in the lotus position (legs crossed and hands held on our knees or in a prayer position), that posture helps the flow of qi through our bodies. It also helps to coalesce and store qi in our bodies. People who meditate universally report that they feel healthier, calmer, and more energetic on the days they meditate than on the days they do not.

No human meditates as well as a cat. Look at

your cat carefully the next time she is "resting."
She usually meditates in the sunshine or near a
fire, absorbing the energy and warmth. During
her meditation, she assumes a special, lotuslike
posture. Her haunches are nestled beneath her.
Her front paws are pressed together beneath her
chest. This posture, like the human lotus position, gathers and stores energy.

The Purr

In some traditions, meditators say a mantra. Although most people think of a mantra as the
"oohmmm" made famous in the 1960s, a mantra
can be any tonal sound that resonates for that
person.

Cats have a mantra that makes any human
mantra seem insignificant: the purr. A sound
that sings with the sweet energy of the universe.
Some cats have loud purrs, sharing their songs
with the world. Others sing quietly to themselves. If you know your cat well, you will notice
that the purr she makes as she meditates has a

distinctly different sound from her purr when she is telling you that she'd appreciate some dinner. It is rhythmic, melodious, and primal.

A purr is more than a mere song. A cat's purr pulses throughout her body, massaging her organs and muscles. It affects the rhythms of blood flow throughout her body, including the flow of blood to her brain.

I occasionally receive treatments from a chiropractor. At the end of the treatments, my chiropractor places a Qi Machine on my lower back. This machine, which was made in China, emits a pulsating, rhythmic throb that is designed to help qi flow through the patient's body. It is sensuous and healing to feel the warm throbbing on my back. However, my chiropractor's Qi Machine is a poor cousin to my cat's pulsating, throbbing, massaging, internal purr.

Cats clearly benefit from their meditation. There is no mistaking the look of contented joy in the closed eyes and soft face of a meditating cat. There can be little doubt that cats also share the longer-term effects of meditation that humans feel: more energy, clearer mind, and calmness.

Follow the example of your cat and meditate daily. Better yet, meditate with your cat. The next time your cat is meditating, lie or sit close beside her. Relax your head, neck, shoulders, arms, chest, back, waist, pelvis, and legs. Close your eyes and concentrate on the sound, the rhythm, and the vibration of your cat's purr. Allow your relaxed body to experience that feeling inside your being. Your cat will gladly share.

The first time I shared my cat's purr was an awe-inspiring moment. It made me feel just a taste of the relaxation and utter contentment that my cat experiences many times every day.

Moving Meditation

A Taoist tradition of moving meditation, known as qigong (pronounced chee-gong), uses slow body movement to move qi through the body. Tai chi is the most recognized form of qigong among westerners.

Cats as Qigong Masters

In qigong, we bring qi through our bodies with slow movements of our arms, neck, back, and legs while our minds are at rest. Taoists call this the movement within the stillness within the movement. (Our bodies are moving, our minds are still, and the energy is moving inside our bodies.)

Many of the movements in qigong are based on the movements of animals, including cranes, turtles, bears, and tigers.

Our cats, of course, have their own forms of qigong. The cats in my life have practiced the following qigong forms daily:

The Scratching Post. Watch the flow of energy through her body when your cat uses her scratching post. Of course, she is sloughing off old nail material so her claws will be sharp. But she's also sloughing off old energy.

Observe her movements. Your cat stretches her spine and extends her front legs as far as they will stretch. Then she digs her feet deep into a satisfying material. She tenses and relaxes the muscles of one paw, foreleg, and shoulder and then the other.

Try it yourself. Reach your arms above your head and then stretch each arm to its limit, clenching and unclenching your fists. Don't stretch like a human: stretch like a cat, with full extension of your fingers, arms, shoulders, and the muscles of your back. You'll feel the energy flow in your hands, arms, shoulders, neck, and back. Imagine how good it feels to a cat to do this motion several times a day.

Grooming. Your cat licks herself to stay clean. She also licks herself to remove the old qi from her body. Our bodies are surrounded by a halo of qi, with fresh qi coming into our pores and old qi leaving.

Watch as your cat grooms herself with her incredible barbed tongue. She's doing much more than just getting oil and grime off her coat. She's massaging her skin. She's also flicking the old qi away with her tongue, allowing the new qi to flow smoothly. Qigong practitioners flick

away old qi with their hands, grasping the air
next to their bodies with their fingertips and
quickly tossing the old qi into the universe in a
manner almost identical to the way cats flick old
qi away with their tongues.

Cats as Yoga Masters

Although yoga was developed in India, it is consistent with the Chinese Taoist tradition of moving meditation and qigong. Some qigong
positions are the same as some yoga poses. Both
forms of meditative exercise allow us to open the
flow of energy throughout our bodies. Both allow the practitioner to be centered, to be quiet,
to come back to balance, to reconnect with his
whole being, and to reconnect to his breathing.
These meditative exercises connect the mind,
body, and spirit.

Most yoga positions involve stretching. This
stretching allows energy to come into the body,
massaging the internal organs. Different posi-

tions create different breathing patterns that are important to the physical and spiritual health of the practitioner.

Cats practice yoga daily. A yoga teacher identified for me nearly twenty specific yoga poses that her cat performs on a regular basis. The following are a few of the poses:

The Cat Pose. Yes, there is a yoga position named after the typical movement of a cat. In this pose, the person has her hands and knees on the floor, and her back is arched, stretching her spine. Cats, of course, do this pose several times a day. When your cat positions herself into a cat pose, she keeps her tail down, adding to the stretch of the spine.

The Extended Child's Pose. In this position, the cat starts out in the cat pose, but then extends her forelegs out in front. This gives greater stretch to the shoulders and front legs.

The Cow Pose. This position is basically the opposite of the cat pose, with the back arched downward toward the earth. When cats do a cow pose, they usually hold their tails up.

The Serpent Pose. In this pose, the cat keeps her back legs lying on the ground and straightens out her front legs, arching her spine downward toward the earth. This pose realigns vertebrae that may be slightly out of place.

The Heron Pose. This is the typical cat grooming pose, with one hind leg held high in the air. The position is believed to be healthy for the leg joints, spine, and kidneys.

The yoga teacher who shared her insights into cat yoga with me said that her cat does yoga with her almost every day. Cats seem to enjoy yoga's quiet time and flow of energy as much as people do.

Whether you label it qigong, yoga, or cat movements, it is a marvel to watch the stretches, energy flow, and grace of movement that our animal companions perform many times each day. Join in with your cat, and feel the qi flow through your body and the exchange of qi between you and your cat.

As you do, you will be linked to the mystery and healing light of the Tao.

Qi and the Art of Communication

We exude qi from our bodies and absorb qi from other things. Every time we exchange energy with another being, we are communicating with that person, animal, or plant.

When we breathe out carbon dioxide that is absorbed into a plant, and that plant emanates oxygen back to us, we are exchanging qi with the plant. When your boss is looking at you sternly, and you are sitting with erect posture and assuring him that the project will be done on time, you are exchanging qi. When you share a glance with an attractive new neighbor, you're definitely exchanging qi.

Although the exchange of qi is the sharing of pure energy, we show many outward signs that the exchange is happening. When we see a friend we smile and wave. We scowl when someone near us is rude. We run up and hug a loved one. These physical reactions are an acknowledgment of the exchange of qi we are experiencing with the other person. In fact, these physical postures enhance the flow of qi between us. When you smile and say hello to someone on the street, you can feel a much stronger sense of that person than if you walk past without a smile or greeting.

We exchange qi with our cats every day. Your cat is much more attuned to signs of the exchange of energy than any human can be. Her amazing whiskers pick up the tiniest change in your heartbeat. Her extraordinary hearing notes the slightest change in your tone of voice. Her sensitive fur and skin can feel the tension in your hand. Her acute sense of smell can detect physiological changes to your body brought on by fear or excitement.

It is no wonder that no human being can get a cat into a carrier on time for a visit to a veterinarian. It is only surprising that humans are always so puzzled that the cat figured out that this was the day of her annual checkup.

Talking to Your Cat

You and your cat are communicating—and exchanging qi—constantly. Your cat can learn to respond to almost anything you say. You just need to be consistent and kind.

Use your cat's name when you speak to her. She'll learn it very quickly. Most cats learn to respond to "kitty." Your cat can easily be taught to respond to the special name that you selected for her with such love.

Give your cat the opportunity to learn and understand her name. Don't use nicknames. If your cat's name is Sally, call her by saying "Here, Sally." Don't confuse her by sometimes saying "Here, little fuzzy face" or "Here, sweet lambie pie."

Use the same words, phrases, and gestures each time you ask your cat to do a particular act. The exchange of qi flows best where there is consistency.

Speak Softly

Cats have soft voices. They respond to us and hear us best when we speak softly. Lower your voice. Whisper.

Listening to Your Cat

You can listen to your cat just as well as you can talk to her. If you pay attention to what your cat is asking of you, then you will be able to respond with what she needs. The more you respond to your cat, the more information she will share. The myth of the aloof cat will be long gone, as you realize just how much your cat really has to say.

The Silent Command

Cats don't need to speak to tell us what they want. The cat who sits and stares at her food dish is giving you a clear message that doesn't require any words. Your cat may gaze at the door to tell you she wants to go outside. She may stare at the water faucet, waiting for the water to come out so she can play with it.

Several times a day, your cat will go to whatever she wants, stare at it, and wait for you to make it happen. If I'm not responding quickly enough to her requests, my cat will lift her right paw into the air as a reminder to hurry. Your cat will likely have a signal for you when you're not responding correctly.

When you give the cat what she asks for, you'll almost always receive a soft, quick murmur—a thank-you.

Think about the magic of this set of events. Your cat is communicating to you exactly what she needs. When you respond, she tells you that you helped her. That is as pure as an energy exchange can be.

Vocalizations

Cats usually don't talk as much as some other creatures. Like other quiet folks, they generally have something to say when they do speak. Different cats have different vocal patterns. Listen to your cat and determine what she is trying to tell you.

It doesn't take a Taoist in tune with the universe to recognize the growls and hisses of an unhappy, frightened cat. Nature designed these defensive systems to be unmistakable to any species.

Your cat's meows, on the other hand, are a much more subtle form of communication. She has a greeting noise. Your cat has a prolonged yowl to demand something right away, such as her supper (or yours). She has a special sound that is her invitation to you to play.

Pay attention to her murmurs, chirps, and mewls. Cats don't speak just to hear themselves talk. The more you learn to associate your cat's sounds with what she wants, the more you can do for your cat. The more her vocalizations have an influence on your behavior, the more your cat will talk to you. Your relationship, and the exchange of qi between the two of you, will flourish and deepen.

Purr

Every cat has a number of different purrs that are distinct and have their own meanings. Your cat has a special purr when she meditates and one she sings to herself when she's sick. She also has a purr that is reserved to communicate her pleasure with you.

Next time you approach your relaxed cat, pay attention to her purr. Your cat may be lying down by herself. You may hear or sense her soft purr. When you stop to gently scratch her under the chin, the volume revs up. She looks at you and purrs loudly to let you know that you're making her happy. She's communicating loudly and clearly. She's giving some of her qi to you.

Body Language

Cats, with their lithe musculature and flowing tails, tell us as much with their bodies as they do through their talking.

Cats have scent glands at the corners of their mouths and just in front of their ears. They rub these glands against objects and creatures they treasure. When a cat rubs her body against yours, she is claiming a special relationship with you. In effect, she is leaving a sign that her qi is mingled with your qi.

Domestic cats are the only cats in the world who are able to hold their tails vertically while walking. There is no happier sight than a cat trotting up to her human companion, tail held high in the air.

Think of the exchange of qi that the cat is presenting to you. She is giving you energy from her face and body, hoping to have that flow of energy reciprocated. When you take the time to greet your friendly kitty, she responds with loving nuzzling. When you ignore the greeting or tell her to get out of your way, she is much less likely in the future to share her energy with you.

Every cat has times when she doesn't want to be disturbed, and she will tell you so. A stern look in her eye, a slight tensing of her muscles, a paw placed on your hands with claws out just far enough to remind you that she has them, a gentle bite to set clear limits—your cat will give you many signals that you're about to do something she finds irritating, uncomfortable, or painful. Respect what your cat is telling you. If you do, she won't need to growl or scratch to make her point.

If you respond to her gentle warning signs, those signs can become symbolic between the two of you. Instead of putting out a paw with claws a bit unfurled, she may progress to just holding up her paw in a particular position.

Every communication between you and your cat involves the exchanging of your energy, your qi. Watch objectively for what your cat is telling you. Also listen with your heart.

Respond in kind to the loving warmth of an upraised tail. Respect the distance your cat is asking for when she tenses her body and turns her head away. Acknowledge the honor a cat is giving to you when she rolls over on her back and asks you to rub her belly. Appreciate her feelings when she tells you not to touch her while she's grooming. When you acknowledge what she says, and respond with love and con-

sideration, your cat will share her very soul with
you.

Telepathy: The Ultimate Exchange of Qi

Cats hold very clear mental pictures of their
thoughts. When a cat is staring at her empty
food dish, waiting for you to fill it, you know
that she visualizes exactly what you want her to
do. When she gazes at the doorknob, telling you
to open it, the picture in her mind is unmistakable.

Countless people have related incidents
where their cats have sent them mental pictures.
It happens too often, and with too much speci-
ficity, to be taken as mere coincidence.

One such incident happened to a friend of
mine. She was on her way to work one morning
and suddenly felt terribly claustrophobic. She
felt as if she were in a closet, even seeing her
clothes hanging above her head. She went home
at lunch, knowing what she was going to find.

Her cat had been inadvertently closed in her closet. She had picked up her animal companion's picture of what was happening.

There is a growing amount of information about communicating with animals through the pictures they give us. Penelope Smith's *Animal Talk: Interspecies Telepathic Communication* (Pegasus Publications, 1989), Beatrice Lydecker's *What the Animals Tell Me* (Harper & Row, 1977), and Lydia Hiby's *Conversations with Animals* (NewSage Press, 1998) explore this topic in depth and give guidance on how to communicate telepathically with your animal companions.

I must admit I was a skeptic about receiving actual pictures until it happened to me. I had always understood my animal companions' body language and their vocalizations well. I knew I had a telepathic relationship with my dogs, since they did their training exercises better when I visualized what I wanted them to do. Still, I had never received a Technicolor vision from an animal and thought perhaps that only happened to the lunatic fringe.

Mews, my cat, changed all that. It happened a few days after I'd adopted her from the local animal shelter. She was scheduled to be spayed the next morning. I had no qualms about the importance of having her spayed but was worried about her going through the pain and trauma of surgery. The night before she was scheduled to go to the veterinarian, I spent extra time with her. I talked to her about the surgery and told her she'd feel better soon. I told her I loved her.

Then Mews, who was still a very wary stray cat, stretched herself out for the first time, so I could see her tummy quite clearly. Her abdomen was shaved and there was a fresh wound across her belly. Mews had obviously been spayed recently. I was surprised but elated; she wouldn't have to go through the surgery. The next morning before taking Mews into the veterinarian, she let me look at her tummy again. I was stunned. Her abdomen wasn't shaved. There was no visible spay scar, recent or otherwise.

I decided to believe the cat was telling me

something. Mews was only about six months old. If she hadn't told me that she was spayed, I would never have assumed that she was. When we arrived at the veterinarian's office, I insisted that he look for a spay scar before anesthetizing Mews. When the veterinarian shaved Mews's tummy, there was a scar. It was well healed; the surgery had taken place at least two months earlier. The veterinarian's assistant looked at me and asked, "How could you possibly have known she was spayed?" I didn't answer her.

If I had not insisted on the veterinarian examining her for a spay scar, the veterinarian would have found the scar only after Mews was anesthetized. She was spared the trauma of anesthesia because, I believe, she showed me that she had already had the surgery.

Telepathic communication is just another form of the exchange of qi among creatures. As children, we seemed to know this was possible. No child is ever surprised that the animals in her books talk.

We have the chance to experience the shamanic ability to talk with and listen to our animals. We shouldn't lose that opportunity just because Western society is cynical and skeptical. Relax your brain and allow yourself the joy of communicating with your cat. You might be surprised to find the dialogue is in three dimensions.

PART TWO

The Innate Nature of the Cat

5

Understanding the Cat

In Taoism, a master is not someone who dominates other creatures or other objects. A master is someone who understands the innate nature of a thing so well that he becomes a part of it. For example, a master boatman knows the water so well that he flows with it.

To have a loving, meaningful relationship with our cats, we need to understand and appreciate the innate nature of our animal companions. Chuang Tzu wrote, "Tigers are a different creature from humans, but you can train them to obey their trainer if you understand how to adapt to them. People who go against the nature of the tiger don't last long."[1]

Of course, a house cat is not a tiger. Making a mistake about the innate nature of a cat has far less dire consequences for the human involved than going against the nature of a tiger. Still, we cannot hope to have a relationship of mutual respect and understanding without delving into the innate nature of our animal companions.

When we understand the innate nature of our animal companions, we can provide them with the environment that appeals to that nature. We can help them be stimulated, satisfied, and content.

Not Just a Little Tiger

A Chinese friend of mine told me the legend of the tiger and the cat. I remember it as follows:

In the beginning, Tiger did not know how to hunt or to take proper care of himself. He went to Cat and said, "Cat, you have so much to teach me. Will you please help?" And so Cat did.

He taught Tiger how to wait patiently and silently for prey and then spring through the air and capture the unsuspecting creature. Cat taught Tiger how to purr.

He taught Tiger to sleep and rest. Cat taught Tiger how to keep himself clean.

Finally Tiger said, "Thank you, Cat, for teaching me these lessons. Now I know everything that you do." With that, Tiger leapt into the air and pounced, intending to turn Cat into dinner.

Cat easily evaded the huge paw of Tiger and climbed up a tree. Cat laughed at Tiger from the top of the tree and said, "I am wiser than you are, Tiger. I did not teach you everything I know. I did not teach you to climb trees."

To this day, Tiger cannot climb a tree.

There is another lesson the domesticated Cat did not teach the Tiger: how to live in a partnership with humans that no wild animal can replicate.

Every book that contains the history of the cat casually says that our feline friends were first domesticated by the early Egyptians. Since the cats were attracted to the rodents that were feeding on Egyptian grain stores, it was natural for cats to become a part of the human household.

When we read these accounts, domestication of the cat appears inevitable. That is absurd. Countless carnivores and omnivores eat rodents. None of the others has come into our homes. Half the households in America don't have a fox nestled on the couch. We have no owl sitting on the windowsill. We don't share our beds with wolverines. Yet these animals are great rodent hunters.

Domestication is a very rare and extraordinary event. It would seem that it's every bit as much about an animal choosing to be with humans as it is about humans wanting the animal in our homes or yards.

There is an enormous distinction between wild animals that are held captive and domestic animals who live in harmony with humans. Wild animals can be raised by humans and bottle-fed. They can be given love and attention and touching every day of their lives. Still, one day that animal will feel the need to be separate from humans.

I once heard a woman who trained raccoons to play basketball interviewed on a public radio program. She said that when raccoons are young, they are very trainable and love to be held by people and to play with them. However, once they reach a certain age, their wild natures take over. I will always remember the woman saying "When they reach this age, they are torn. They will look at me as if to say 'I love you. But I must bite you. But I love you. But I must bite you.'"

Domestication is not just a matter of time. If you take a wild animal into your house, there is little likelihood that his progeny will end up domesticated. Out of all the herd animals, only a tiny handful were domesticated. A smaller fraction of birds have come to live in harmony with humans. And only two predators, domestic dogs and domestic cats, share our homes.

Moreover, scientific study into the genetic

material of domestic animals indicates that domestication is a rare and extraordinary event. Extensive scientific studies have been conducted on the DNA of cattle, chicken, and dogs to determine their genetic ancestry. It has been determined that there were only two domestication events for cattle, one for chickens, and two for dogs. It is believed that all the cattle in the world are descended from just two females, all the chickens from a single hen, and all the dogs from just two female wolves.

Although these studies were not performed on cats, it is possible that somewhere in Egypt, an extraordinary cat must have met an extraordinary person. This cat was different from all the other wild cats who were hunting the rodents in the granaries. This cat wanted to be a friend to humans. She didn't have the same wild side that compelled her to bite or flee from people. She made the rare and extraordinary choice to join us. She taught her kittens to be the same. Because of her choice, our lives are fundamentally different.

Practical Application of the Tao: Spending Time with Your Cat

Cats are domestic companions who crave our time, attention, and touch. Many people assume that cats are naturally aloof, so the animals need no interactions from humans. Of course the cats who live with those people are aloof—and also lonely and most probably very frightened. Those cats are not receiving the touch and attention that they need to be happy household members.

People who are closely tuned in to their cats know how close their animal companions are to them. A woman I know described a time when she was sick as a child. When her mother found out the cat was in the girl's bed, the mother took the cat out of the house. Later no one could find the cat. That afternoon the local grade school called up: The cat was sitting in the child's desk. That cat knew her place was with my friend. When she wasn't allowed there, she did the best she could to be close.

Give your animal companion enough attention to satisfy his need to be with you. Of course, cats don't want constant attention. They ask you not to disturb them when they are grooming or when they are playing certain hunting games. Still, your cat wants your love and affection every day.

Spend at least an hour over the span of a day (a few minutes at a time) caressing, grooming, playing with, and talking with your cat. Scratch under his chin and down his throat. A cat has most of his acupressure points on his head and spine, so be sure to rub those areas to stimulate the flow of healing energy throughout his body.

Cats have scent glands at the corners of their lips and in front of their ears. They rub their faces along anything and anyone they want to lay claim to. Include lots of opportunities for your cat to nuzzle you with his face. It's his way of bonding with you.

Your cat needs that time and physical contact with you every day. Domestic cats who receive this time and attention will be healthier and live longer.

Practical Application of the Tao: Teaching Cats to Enjoy Human Touch

Not all cats like petting. Animals who have been neglected or abused can find a human hand unpleasant or frightening. Work with your petting-averse cat to give him the human bond that he deserves.

Many cats enjoy petting for a brief period of time and then turn on their humans and nip them, saying very clearly "I've had enough." Cats have very sensitive skin and, for some cats, too much petting becomes irritating or painful.

If you have a cat who enjoys petting but then suddenly bites you, pay attention to how long the cat allows you to touch him before he snaps. Then pet him for about half that length of time. So if your animal companion usually bites you after you've stroked him for about a minute, next time pet him for only thirty seconds.

Gradually increase the amount of time you pet him. By doing so, you may be able to desensitize his skin so he will enjoy longer and longer petting sessions.

Always respect his warnings to you that he has had enough. Stop stroking him if he pins his ears back, gently puts out his claws, or otherwise communicates to you that you need to stop. If you ignore his warnings, he will trust you less each time you come into contact with him.

Lao Tzu wrote:

> In the universe great acts are made up of
>   small deeds,
> The sage does not attempt anything very
>   big,
> And thus achieves greatness.[2]

With any behavior problem you face with your cat, dealing with small incremental steps is the pathway to solving even the most difficult problem.

Abandoned and Stray Cats

It is common for abandoned and stray cats to be petting-averse. When I first brought home my cat, Mews, from my local shelter, she was nervous with any extended petting.

Although Mews was obviously a purebred Persian, life apparently had not always been handed to her on a silver platter. She had been brought in as a stray who was hanging around someone's yard. She was emaciated. She had such a bad case of ear mites that she had bleeding sores behind her ears where she was digging at her skin, trying to alleviate the itching. Her filthy coat was full of flea dirt. She had worms. Her chronic diarrhea lasted more than a month. At some point someone had obviously given up trying to keep her coat brushed, so she had been shaved down to the skin. All in all, she looked to me like she'd been through a concentration camp.

I spend at least an hour every day with her (a few minutes at a time), stroking her, grooming her, and playing with her. When she first saw a brush, she cried out in fear, so I used a comb to groom her. At first she would only allow the comb to touch her back. Then we progressed to her sides. Now she'll allow a quick swipe at her chest, legs, and even her tummy.

When I first got Mews, she would butt her head against me and allow me to scratch her back gently, but she would pull away nervously from any extended petting. Now she enjoys a leisurely massage on any place except her tummy.

Every day we continue to make progress. While I caress her, I touch her tummy lightly, teaching her it won't hurt if my hand is there.

Mews still resists being picked up but is allowing me to hold her for longer increments of time before she tells me she is too nervous to accept it any longer. She's just beginning to walk across my body but won't curl up in my lap yet. I believe that Mews already trusts me; she is just learning how a cat who trusts people acts.

By spending several short periods of time each day, gently expanding Mews's zone of comfort, she is changing from a semiwild cat to a very domesticated one. Unlike a true wild animal, that transition into tame is permanent. She is relaxing and learning to be the creature that her innate nature wants her to be.

If you have a cat who is aloof or a rescued animal companion who skulks in the corners, work with him just a little bit each day. Expand his comfort zone continually. Soon you will see a noticeable relaxation as he becomes what a cat should be: happy to be alone—but equally happy to be with you.

Feral Cats

A feral cat isn't just a stray. Feral cats live as wild animals. They hunt or scavenge their own food. They live, breed, and die with no help and no interventions from humans.

Scholarly treatises on cat behavior proclaim that a cat who hasn't had human handling by the age of seven weeks will never bond to humans. However, people with extensive experience working with feral cats prove, on a daily basis, that laboratory research is not the best place to learn about the nature of cats. Feral cats can learn to bond with humans and can sometimes make a transition to contented companion animals.

Feral cats, living on the streets or in the fields, need to be given a reason to trust humans. Although feral cats are predators, hunting mice, birds, and other small game, they are also prey animals and are hunted by dogs, coyotes, hawks, raccoons, and humans who don't want a wild cat in the yard. The world is a frightening, dangerous place for feral cats. It is no wonder that they view humans as predators, not as friends.

Still, there is a part of every feral cat that is drawn to humans. Most feral cats can develop a loving bond with humans, if the people are patient enough to allow that bond to happen.

Start slowly by becoming a reliable food source for your wild friend. Over time, give the cat opportunities to eat closer and closer to you. Feed him from your hand.

When he begins to trust you as a provider of

food, hold out your hand, giving him an invitation to nuzzle his face against your finger or to place his back in position to be scratched. Gradually extend those brief bits of contact as the cat allows you.

Quick movements will frighten a feral cat. If you are nervous about your encounter, he will sense it and stay away from you. When you interact with a feral cat, put yourself into a Taoist meditative state. Let yourself be silent and gentle, like a healthy, relaxed cat. Breathe deeply and slowly. The wild cat will be attracted to your calmness.

It may take months of regular effort, but many feral cats can bond with humans. Some can make the transition into becoming indoor cats. A once-feral cat will always be wary of new people. He may not be as quick to snuggle as a cat who had contact with humans as part of his earliest experiences.

While your once-feral cat may not bond with you in the way you expect, he can be a loving friend nonetheless. You just have to respect the kind of bond that particular cat is able and willing to give.

Each feral cat who makes the step from living as a wild creature to one who shares his life with a human is retracing the steps of the first domestic cat. It is a process full of magic and wonder. No wild creature who did not have a need within his inherent nature to be part of the human world would ever make that transition.

Animal Friends

Cats seek out the company of humans. They also seek out the company of other animals.

All species of wild cats, except for lions, are nonsocial creatures who live out a solitary existence. Domestic cats are very different. As long as there is enough available food, feral cats live in colonies. They sleep together. They groom each other. The females take care of each other's kittens. It is the innate nature of most cats to have feline friends.

Cats usually get along well with, and play

with, friendly, safe dogs. One of my dogs came to join my household when my cat, Silver Lining, was quite elderly. The two became fast friends. Silver Lining would go up to Radar, snuggle, and begin to groom him. Radar would reciprocate by studiously licking out her ears. At first I was afraid that Silver Lining was upset with Radar; she had an odd look on her face as his tongue snaked into her ears. When I got closer, I heard Silver Lining's loudest purr. She seemed to be saying "Nobody's done this for me since Mom."

A friend of mine runs a rural animal shelter. Her country home is a peaceable kingdom full of cats, dogs, horses, llamas, birds, goats, and other creatures who were abandoned by humans. We were relaxing in her yard when a big cat came running at my six-pound dog, Goldie. Goldie let out a ferocious (for her) bark and started chasing the cat. The big cat watched Goldie over his shoulder as he loped away, easily keeping just a step ahead of the little dog. When the cat had left the yard, Goldie came back to me, wagging her tail, visibly proud of herself. My friend smiled and said, "Isn't it amazing how the animals always seem to know just what the other ones need?" It was true: The big, savvy barn cat knew he had nothing to fear from the tiny, shy dog. He chose to give the little dog just a moment of fun.

Many cats are playmates with such diverse animals as horses, parakeets, and rabbits. Your cat may not be the life of the party, but it is definitely in his nature to have friends.

6

PLAYING AND HUNTING

Kittens may be the most playful creatures on earth. But play does not end at the age of three months, or three years, or thirteen years. Throughout their lives, cats love to play.

Taoists revel in joyful play. Motion is integral to the Tao. In fact, the Tao itself is said to be ever-present and in motion. So, life itself is motion, exercise, and play.

There is a Chinese saying, "Flowing water never rots." The motion of a flowing stream is a powerful symbol of Taoism, with its gentle, inexorable, sparkling vitality. Cats, perhaps the most playful of beings, reflect this joyful motion.

A well-fed cat allowed outdoors will hunt mice but may play with them and bat them in the air rather than kill them. Many years ago I had a cat named Learned Paw. A cricket appeared in the tiny apartment where I was living at the time. Learned Paw swiftly caught it. Rather than killing the bug, he just broke one of the poor creature's legs. Learned Paw would play with the cricket for a while and then stuff the bug into a corner of a bookcase. He then retrieved the cricket later to play again. I couldn't stand seeing the cricket suffer, so I killed the poor thing. For several days Learned Paw would go to the spot where he had kept the cricket and yowl mournfully.

Cats are sentient beings. They know the difference between batting a ball around the floor and hunting a rodent for dinner. They bat the ball because it is part of their innate nature to play. When your cat stalks your shoelace, she knows it's a game. Your cat doesn't confuse a feathered cat toy with a real bird. She just likes to play with her toy.

Although cats hunt alone, they often play together. Cats will chase their cat or dog friends around the house and will turn around and let themselves be chased. Another cat's tail or a dog's tail is too much fun to resist a pounce. Your newspaper, panty hose, or pen are delightful playthings.

Mews, my cat, and Radar, one of my dogs, love to chase flying insects together. When Mews first joined us, she looked rather askance at Radar when he flitted throughout the house with her in hot pursuit of a fly. Now they play their hunting game happily together. The only conflict is that Mews often eats the bug she catches. Radar whines in frustration because Mews has ended the game.

To satisfy the innate nature of your cat, she needs to play daily. Cats will play by themselves, but they are unhappy if that is the only choice available to them. Because play is a social activity for a cat, it is important that you play games with your animal companion every day.

There are countless interactive toys you can purchase or make for your cat. Most cats are thrilled when their human companions flick a feather around, inviting a game of chase. A large percentage of cats enjoy playing fetch with small balls, crumpled paper, or other little objects. Chasing a string across the floor or pouncing on any object that wiggles underneath a newspaper is enormous fun.

Let your cat teach you the games she likes to play. Learned Paw invented a complicated game with rules. For him, chasing a little ball that two humans rolled back and forth was much too simple. Instead, he would hide underneath the couch when we rolled the ball and would pounce on it only when it was in a narrow "strike zone." His challenging game was more fun for him and it was also fun for the two humans.

Mews likes to "hunt" feathers that I jiggle around her scratching posts. Sometimes she finds the way I'm placing the feather less than ideal, so she gently taps her paw just where she wants the feather to dance. I place the feather where she taps her foot, and she happily pounces on her "prey."

When you play games with your cat, you are satisfying her innate nature. You are also sharing a moment of happiness together, exchanging your blissful qi. It is a golden time for both of you to share.

The Ferocity of the Hunt

Cats are hunters of legendary ferocity. When a cat hunts, she rediscovers that portion of her nature that is a small, wild tiger.

Cats have been compared to sharks in the efficiency with which Nature designed their bodies for hunting. Their canine teeth are sensitive and can actually feel delicate sensations, so cats can find the perfect place to bite the neck of a small rodent for an instant kill. Their claws are formidable weapons. Unlike other predators, cats' eyes are designed for round-the-clock hunting.

One of the great wonders of this planet is the beauty of watching a cat hunt. The cat will wait silently, without moving a muscle, for prey to come into view. Then there is the leap and the swipe of a paw. Both paws come together. A cat is so swift and so sure that a fly can be caught between her paws. Then it is over as quickly as it began, a dance of pure yang energy.

Hunting and Qi

Cats willingly put their paws into holes in the ground. They play by sticking their feet into paper bags or under blankets. I once said to a friend of mine, "Isn't it amazing that cats will blindly put their paws into strange places? If something happened to seriously injure his paws, a wild cat would die of starvation. It seems that Nature would tell cats not to place their feet somewhere the cat can't see." My friend replied, "What makes you think the cat doesn't know exactly what's in the hole or under the blanket? Just because we can't see what's there doesn't mean the cat can't see it."

She was right. Cats hunt largely by feeling the qi of the creatures they hunt. They don't need their extraordinary eyes to know the location of a fly in the air or a mouse in a hole.

Practical Application of the Tao: Focusing Ferocity

A cat who doesn't have enough outlets for her ferocious energies will focus them on her human companions. She will pounce on ankles. She will attack you in your sleep. She will shred your skin with her claws. She'll stalk you as you come up the stairs or as you brush your teeth. Although the cat may be enjoying herself, it is not the Tao of the human to be cat prey. Too much

stalking from our cats deteriorates our relationship with each other and reduces the flow of qi.

Ferocity is pure yang energy. Your cat needs
some outlet for her hunting nature or the yang
energy will build up inside her, causing her to
become overly aggressive. Consistent, regular
play is important, because bored cats store up
their yang energy and cannot curb the ferocity
they feel.

A cat's yang nature can also build up on itself.
It is easy for a cat to get out of control, out of
balance with her ferocity. When a cat is experiencing too much yang energy, she loses her yin
side. You must provide play opportunities for
your cat that balance out her yin and yang natures.

Focus your cat's energy on gentle play. Play
is hunting without the ferocity. Playing games
with you, other cats, or other household animals
will blunt the edge of her fierceness. Be sure that
your cat gets plenty of chances to run, chase,
pounce, and bite in play. Then she won't need to
do it in earnest.

If your cat is in the habit of stalking you, take a toy with you and let her attack the toy. Mews went through a stage in which she waited at the top of the stairs, pouncing on the dogs and me as we unsuspectingly walked up to the bedroom. I began to carry a big feather with me when I went upstairs. I'd jiggle the feather around and she'd catch the feather instead of my flesh. Soon her predatory behavior changed to a play behavior. Now she waits at the top of the stairs and leaps into the air, a new game we share. The ferocity was redirected and blunted.

Beware of games that cross over from play to ferocity. Many people allow their cats to grab their hands, with back feet kicking. This is a game kittens play, teaching each other the skills of defensive fighting. The powerful thrust of back legs against an opponent's vulnerable underside can save a cat from an aggressor. When you allow your cat to play this game, the play can turn in an instant into a real battle for your feline friend. You've become an aggressor in her mind, deteriorating your relationship. Instead of playing the game with your hand, give your cat a large, catnip-filled toy to play aggression-defense games.

Whenever your cat's eyes dilate and become glazed and her ears curve against her head, either focus her energy on a toy or cut off contact. Do not allow her ferocity to change your relationship with her.

In a household, it is the human's responsibility to direct and focus the qi of all the creatures who live there. Redirecting your cat's ferocity into play will change discord into harmony. Your cat, any other creatures in the house, and you will all benefit.

7

INDOOR VERSUS OUTDOOR CATS

We all struggle about what is best for our cats: life entirely spent indoors or life that includes the outdoors.

Taoists have a reverence for long life. That would indicate that cats should live indoors. The average life expectancy of an outdoor cat is about three years. Most indoor cats can expect to live well into their teens.

On the other hand, Taoists also respect Nature and the natural functions of every animal. Thus it can be argued that cats were designed to hunt and should be allowed the freedom of the outdoors.

Dangers of the Outdoors

There is little that is natural in the great outdoors of urban streets. Nature did not design cats to withstand the impact of an automobile. City cats belong inside the safety of a home.

Suburban and even rural areas also can be deadly. Because humans have decimated so many prey animals, predators such as coyotes, raccoons, and even hawks frequently turn to cats as a source of food.

I knew a woman who had a gentle, declawed little Himalayan cat. The woman and the cat lived in a condominium in the city, where the cat was strictly an indoor companion. When the woman moved to the country, she decided her cat needed to experience the "natural" environment. She literally had to push the cat out the door. It wasn't long before the cat was never seen again. She was almost certainly a meal for one of the hungry coyotes who occasionally came through the woman's country property.

Most quiet, friendly house cats are likely to be prey rather than predator in the real outdoors. For most cats and most situations, the best home is safely inside.

Practical Application of the Tao: Creating an Indoor Life

Indoors is just a dreary prison for a cat unless his human companion makes a conscious effort to make the home a joyful, fun-filled place. Indoor space is yin in nature. It is important that you provide opportunities for your cat to express his yang side. Otherwise he will become either overly passive or overly aggressive. The activities available for your cat must be varied. He must have opportunities to exert his innate nature, which includes his need for companionship, his playfulness, and his ferocity. The environment must also appeal to his intelligence.

Scratching Posts

Every cat home needs scratching posts. Posts must be high enough for a cat to reach up and really stretch out his whole body while kneading with his paws. Different cats prefer different types of surfaces on a post. If your cat doesn't play with traditional carpet-covered posts, try sisal, cardboard, and natural wood. For your cat to be content indoors, he needs to be able to stretch and scratch.

Toys and Games that Simulate Rodent Hunting

It is in the innate nature of a cat to hunt rodents, crouching silently for the perfect moment and then pouncing suddenly. Make sure your cat has the chance to physically simulate rodent hunting. Toys that do this include balls that he bats around, round tubes into which the cat sticks his paw to push a ball, and strings or feathers that you draw across the ground. Consciously imitate the movements that a rodent might make when you play with the cat. Make sure your string "hides" in a plant or behind the scratching post. Scratch your fingers underneath a blanket, like a small burrowing mouse. Think like a rodent so your cat has the chance to think like a cat.

Toys and Games that Simulate Bird Hunting

It is the innate nature of cats to hunt birds, just as it is their nature to hunt rodents. Give your cat the chance to leap and swat, since his body must make those motions to feel complete. Tie a string to a rod and put feathers at the end of the string. Let the toy swoop above your cat's head. Think and move like a bird. Most of our homes are host to the occasional fly or moth. These bird substitutes can help meet a cat's innate need to hunt.

Perches

Cats love to watch the action outside. If your windowsills are narrow, be sure the cat has a roomy perch by at least one window in every room. When I look at Mews gazing out the window watching birds, I am convinced that she is content to be inside. She reminds me of a person who likes to watch sports on television; she enjoys just looking and fantasizing.

Water Games

Cats enjoy the movement and flow of water. Let your feline friend play with the water from a faucet or fountain. Consider a fish aquarium, as long as the fish are well-protected and aren't made to feel like prey.

Fresh Air

All creatures need fresh air. Put sturdy screens on your windows and doors that will withstand a cat leaning against them. Some cats will even pounce into screens, hanging suspended with all four sets of claws stuck securely into the screening. As long as you are sure your screens are sturdy, it is important to keep windows open in nice weather to allow your indoor cat some air.

Consider purchasing or making a totally enclosed outdoor space for your cat. Window boxes that fit in apartments or condos can give your cat a safe taste of the outdoors. If you have a house with a yard, consider building or buying fencing (including a top) for your patio or yard so your animal companion can jump and play in a safe, enclosed area outdoors.

Going for Walks

Many cats can be trained to walk on a leash. Although some cats adapt to walking in strange, busy, places, most prefer a stroll in their own backyard.

To train your cat to walk on a leash, first introduce him to a cat harness. Make this a gradual process that can take several weeks. Let your animal companion sniff the harness. Keep the harness in plain sight so your cat can become accustomed to it. Then gently lay it against your cat's body while you stroke or groom him. Over time, gradually increase the length of time your cat has the harness draped across his back. Begin putting the strap around his tummy. After he is comfortable with the feel of the harness on his body, loosely fasten the buckles or hooks. Eventually, secure the strap around his girth more and more tightly, until it is tight enough for your cat to walk safely outside.

Once your cat has the harness on his body, allow him to walk around the house, with you holding the leash and following him. After he is very comfortable with that, begin to introduce him to the backyard in his harness.

Never try to pull your cat. If you want him to go in a certain direction, coax him with lots of talk and a cat treat.

If your cat likes his outings with you in the backyard, you can try taking him other places to see if he enjoys those experiences as well. Most cats would rather stay in their familiar territory, but some cats have an adventurous streak and enjoy going new and different places with their human companions.

Time

Cats can and do live happy, fulfilled lives indoors. They can do so only when we make sure their innate natures have the chance to express themselves. Cats who live indoors need more time and attention from their human companions than cats who spend time outdoors. Their humans become focal points for their lives. You have an obligation to give your cat the love, intellectual stimulation, physical activity, and time that provides him a meaningful life inside.

Practical Application of the Tao: The Outside Cat

For the four millennia cats have lived with humans, most felines have been allowed to spend time outside. Obviously they can live a long and healthy life if all goes well. In making a decision about whether your cat will be happy and safe outside, think about his strength, his prey drive, his life story, and your surroundings.

Cats Who Must Not Go Outside

There are some situations in which a cat must never go outside. Declawed cats cannot protect themselves from dogs, other cats, or predators. They must never leave the safety of your home.

If you live in an urban area with busy streets, you are sentencing your cat to death if you let him out the door. If you live in an area in which many wild animals have been pushed from their natural habitats and are hunting for food, your cat is not likely to live long. Because of human intervention into the natural order of things, in these situations a cat cannot rely on his abilities to keep himself safe.

Cats Who May Do Well Outdoors

Just as there are some cats who must surely never go outdoors, there are some cats who do well in a life that includes going outdoors some or even all of the time. I have a friend who has five barn cats who are all several years old. This animal-loving woman says, "I don't think that most cats belong outside. But every one of these cats has a story, and I can't imagine these particular cats doing well inside."

Cats who do well outdoors have a number of traits in common.

Exposed to Outdoor
Life Since Kittenhood

Mother cats teach their kittens how to survive in their environments. Kittens learn from their mothers how to hunt and how to take care of themselves in the outdoors. Unless they learn these lessons from their mothers, kittens probably will not mature into capable outdoor cats.

Everyone has seen, or at least read about, mother cats teaching their kittens to hunt. The mother brings her kittens mice and other game to practice upon. Mother cats give other life lessons to their kittens as well.

One woman I know reported that she had a cat who would take every litter of her kittens out to the side of the road. The mother cat would carry each kitten into the street, one by one, then smack the kitten's head with her powerful paw. Mother cat got the message across loud and clear: Roads are dangerous places. Cats with mothers who teach them about the dangers of the environment are much more likely to survive than those whose mothers don't teach them.

Strong Prey Drive

Some cats have an extreme prey drive and seek out the excitement of the hunt. They quickly tire of human-made cat games. They chatter and quiver as they watch birds through the window. They are escape artists. They knock glasses off the counter for the excitement of watching them break. They stalk their human companions mercilessly, often attacking them as they sleep. These keen, prey-oriented cats may benefit from the chance to use their instincts fully, as long as they were raised by a mother cat who taught them how to cope with the outdoors.

Strong Bodies

The toughest cat in the world will not survive a meeting with a car. However, the bigger and stronger the cat, the more likely he is to survive run-ins with other cats, dogs, raccoons, and other predators. If you have a sweet, gentle, longhaired cat, he is not going to live long outside. If you have a tough twenty-pound alley cat, he may thrive in the right outdoor environment.

Safe Surroundings

If your cat is allowed outside either part time or all the time, his territory must be as safe as you can make it. He needs to have places that he can jump up to in order to get out of the way of dogs or other predators. He needs to have clean bedding, free of fleas, in a place that is warm and secure.

Just because an animal lives outside, we humans are not freed of our responsibility for his care. We have created an environment in which game is scarce and diseases can thrive. Every cat deserves full preventive medical care as well as response to medical emergencies. The cat must have a regular supply of food and fresh water, given to him in a place that other cats, dogs, raccoons, or coyotes cannot invade. Because even outdoor cats are domestic creatures, he needs your attention and affection. He craves a bond with you, even though that bond may be somewhat different from the bond with an indoor cat.

Making the Right Decision

I have known cats who have lived long, healthy lives partially or entirely outdoors. I also have known cats whose lives were cut sadly short because they were allowed outside and did not have the tools to cope with the demands of the environment.

Throughout my adult life, my cats have been indoor cats. I cannot judge how much my animal companions have missed because they were not allowed outside to hunt for real rodents and birds. On the other hand, I have never faced the guilt and heartache of a cat who has been killed by a car, injured in a cat fight, wounded by a dog, or exposed to feline leukemia or feline immunodeficiency virus.

In this difficult human world we have created, we must weigh and balance very carefully what is the right living environment for each cat. Consider the environment around you and the innate nature of your individual cat as you make that decision on behalf of another creature.

8

Cats are rooted to the earth through their love of territory. Look at a cat when she enters a new place: body close to the ground, paws gripping the floor. She has lost all of her airy yang energy and is solely a creature of earthy yin energy.

Your cat can feel comfortable and secure — balanced between yin and yang — only if she has a territory that feels safe to her. Her territory allows your cat to relax her hold on the earth. It brings her back to her natural balance.

Perhaps the most important way you can contribute to your cat's sense of well-being is to provide her with a territory that feels safe to her and is in concert with her innate nature.

Many common problems faced by people who live with cats, including litter box problems, spraying, and even aggression, can be linked to a cat's insecurity about her territory.

A Cat's Sacred Place

A cat's territory is her sacred space. It is where she finds her food. It is the place where she can sleep in peace. It is her safe haven. Because our cats live with us, they do not have the freedom of choice to find a territory of their own. Thus it is our responsibility to ensure that our cat's living space is clean, safe, and tranquil.

Cruelty-Free Home

Your cat's home must be a cruelty-free place. No one should be allowed to harm the cat in any way. This means no physical "discipline." Physical punishment teaches a cat nothing and only frays her relationship to the humans in her life.

Some cats are quite content to be dressed up as a child's "baby doll" and carted through the house. For others, this treatment is torture. Children can learn the different ways individual cats should be treated. It's an opportunity for your children to learn the value of every living creature.

Sharing Territory

People, like cats, cherish their own territories. Lao Tzu wrote:

> People follow earth,
> earth follows heaven,
> heaven follows the Way
> the Way follows what is.[1]

So, like our cats, it is our Tao (Way) to feel close to our physical place on this earth.

Therefore, it is perfectly correct for the humans in the household to set limits on the cat's territory, as long as those limits are clear and enforced consistently and without physical punishment. If you do not want the cat on the counter, put two-sided tape on the forbidden surface, so the cat learns the counter is an undesirable part of her territory. Lock cabinet doors rather than yell at a cat or hit her for following her natural curiosity and exploring behind closed doors.

Cats have a right to live without fear of injury from other animals. Most cats enjoy the company of other cats (if properly introduced). Many dogs and cats become lifelong companions. However, if one animal threatens the safety or the tranquillity of another, it is best to find a new home for one of the animals. Every creature deserves to feel safe in his own home.

Nontoxic Environment

Be sure that you keep your home free of plants that are toxic to cats. Keep chemicals and medicines locked up. Your home is also your cat's home. She has a right to a territory that is not toxic or poisonous. No matter how beautiful a plant may be or how handy a chemical may be, it does not belong in a cat's home if it might hurt her.

Clean Surroundings

Cats, of course, don't care if the laundry is a little behind schedule. (They like to sleep on your clothes both before and after the wash.) They do care if their kitty litter box is dirty. It is a cat's nature to use clean areas for elimination. She cannot do that without human help. Every litter box should be cleaned at least once a day (at least twice a day if there is more than one cat using the box). There should be at least one kitty litter box on each story of your house, and no more than two cats per litter box. Unclean litter is repugnant to a cat and makes her feel uncomfortable in her own home.

Tranquillity

Cats are peaceful, quiet creatures. They can be content only in peaceful, quiet surroundings. If there is a lot of yelling and dissension in your home, your cat will be nervous in her environment and may well act out in an aggressive manner. She may mark her territory by scratching with her claws or with urine marking to reinforce her place in a household full of uncertainty.

If your home is happy but noisy, a cat can still be content, but she will need a quiet place to relax away from the melee. This may be her own bed tucked into a quiet corner of the house. It's just as likely to be a place that she selects. As long as the place is warm, soft, and quiet, your cat can relax while the rest of the household rushes through its busy routine.

There is a lesson for all of us in this. If we doubt whether our home is a safe, tranquil haven for our cats, it is obviously not a good place for us either. To experience the peace and joy that the Tao provides, we all need to have a place that is safe and healing.

Cats and Feng-Shui

A cat who is comfortable in her territory makes that space her own. She creates a positive qi field that makes the home a better place for all of us to live.

The Taoist art and science of feng-shui is the study of how our living and working spaces affect our lives. People knowledgeable about feng-shui can analyze the energy flows in the land and use it to design space that is in harmony with that energy flow.

For people who love cats, their animal companions are an important element of feng-shui, since cats bring such positive energy to a space. Houses, with their close relationship to the ground, are yin spaces. A cat's yang energy as he plays brings a yin/yang harmony to his home. Cats move stagnant energy with their play and activity. They attract good energy with their meditative ways.

So, as we provide a safe, tranquil home for our cats, they in turn make our homes warmer, more inviting, and more serene.

PART THREE

Wu Wei:
Powerful
Nonaction

9

THE PRINCIPLE OF WU WEI

The least action is the best action. This principle, known as wu wei (pronounced woo way), is a basic tenet of Taoism. Usually it is illustrated by a small stream and a huge boulder. Humans may use massive equipment and a huge effort to try to move a boulder, but it still may be impossible to make the boulder budge. However, a tiny stream can defeat the might of the boulder. The stream quietly skirts around the boulder's edges and still gets to where it wants to go. Eventually the stream will erode the boulder, and the mighty rock will yield to the tiny stream.

Lao Tzu wrote in the *Tao Te Ching:*

Under heaven nothing is more soft and
    yielding than water,
Yet for attacking the solid and strong,
    nothing is better;

It has no equal.

The weak can overcome the strong;

The supple can overcome the stiff.[1]

Wu wei is often called the action of nonaction. True power comes from the gentle quietness of the stream, not from mighty struggles to move the rock.

Just as a cat could well symbolize the balance of yin and yang, a cat also could symbolize the nonaction of wu wei. Most cats sleep about eighteen hours a day. Compared to any other predator species, they seem to do nothing except rest and groom themselves. Yet cats can catch so much prey that they can decimate a wild area. Mother cats relax languidly with their kittens but also teach them to hunt, keep them groomed, and take the time to play with them. With no visible effort, cats gently take over our homes, usually ruling other animals under the roof, including humans, without anyone ever noticing their power.

The Book of Chuang Tzu tells us:

One who follows the Tao daily does
less and less. As he does less and less, he
eventually arrives at actionless action.
Having achieved actionless action, there
is nothing which is not done.[2]

What better description is there of a cat? He
apparently does nothing, yet nothing is left un-
done.

Stillness

To achieve wu wei, we must be still. This includes the stillness of meditation. It also includes
stillness in how we conduct our daily lives. We
must be silent to hear the rhythms of the universe.

The Book of Chuang Tzu says:

The sages are quiescent, not because of
any value in being quiescent, they simply
are still. Not even the multitude of beings
can disturb them, so they are calm. . . .

Empty, still, calm, plain, quiet, silent, actionless action is the foundation of all life.[3]

It is the cat's stillness that allows him to hear the vibrations of a mouse's feet. It is his silence that makes him successful in stalking his prey. It is his quietness that permits him to feel the energy of a fly between his paws. It is his hours of rest that give him the energy to spring into the air with the grace and strength of an eagle.

Motion begins with stillness.

Softness

Just as wu wei requires stillness, it also requires softness. I had the privilege of attending a retreat where an internationally famous qigong master, Dr. Liu Dong, came to share his form of qigong and his Taoist beliefs. Master Liu spoke a lot about softness. He said, "Those who appear soft on the outside are the strongest on the inside. We do not put our energy into being hard, so we flow with the current. Just like a soft willow tree lasts through the storm that knocks over a strong oak tree, so the soft are able to withstand more, and last longer, than the hard."

There is no creature softer than a cat. Cats have light, silken fur. The contours of their heads and bodies are round. When they are re- laxed, their muscles feel so soft that they seem to be made of rags.

Still, pound for pound, there may be no stronger creature. Often a cat can fight off a dog ten times his size, using hard talons that are nor- mally sheathed inside little, soft paws.

Cats have soft voices. They conserve their en- ergy in their softness.

One of the great lessons we can learn from our cats is the secret of wu wei. Cats are stronger because of their softness. They are more effective because of their rest. They con- trol those around them far more by the power of their presence than they could ever do with force. These small companion animals are more powerful than most large creatures.

Cats and the Use of Force

Lao Tzu wrote:

> Whenever you advise a ruler in the way
>   of the Tao,
> Counsel him not to use force to conquer
>   the universe.
> For this would only cause resistance.

The passage concludes:

> Force is followed by loss of strength.
> This is not the way of Tao.
> That which goes against the Tao comes to
>   an early end.[1]

Any human who has been foolish enough to try to punish an angry cat physically knows this cannot be the way of Tao. In fact, at times such as this we are reminded of Chuang Tzu's ad-

monishment that people who go against the nature of the tiger don't last long. Those who
follow the principle of wu wei refrain from
force.

Punishing a cat only produces more resistance. Screaming, shouting, hitting, or other violent actions will not improve your cat's behavior.
If you act this way, your cat may respond by
biting or scratching you. She will always respond by lessening her trust in you, reducing the
precious flow of qi between the two of you.

When trying to change a cat's behavior, it is
far easier to direct your energy to the problem
rather than to the cat. Thus, stop a cat from
scratching the furniture by making the furniture
unattractive to the cat. Solve the problem of a
cat jumping on the counter by making the
counter unappealing. For example, cover your
furniture with a blanket or throw that does not
give the cat the traction he needs to scratch.
Placing two-sided tape or aluminum foil on a
countertop makes the surface undesirable to a
cat. You will not have to force him to stop claw-

ing the couch or leaping onto the countertop. Because you have made these surfaces unattractive, the cat will decide for himself to leave them alone.

The principle of wu wei tells us the path of least resistance is the best path. The wise person realizes that it is much easier to alter the environment than to confront the claws of a cat directly.

Practical Application of the Tao: Using the Principle of Wu Wei to Train Your Cat

Contrary to years of Western-based thought, cats are trainable. By appealing to the innate nature of our cats, we can teach them much. If we do it right, training is highly enjoyable for the cat.

Western-based dominance methods of training do not work. Punishment just creates aggression. Cats are not impressed when their

entire reward for a job well done is a brief moment of praise.

However, cats do enjoy solving puzzles, find-
ing delicious food, and playing with their human
companions. Using the principle of wu wei, you
can work with what your cat enjoys to teach her
the actions that you want her to follow.

If you reward your cat with a taste of her
favorite food as well as lots of petting and praise
when she does what you ask, your animal companion will learn quickly. Training exercises will
be an enjoyable game for her and part of the
bonding experience that the two of you share.
You'll notice that your cat is purring and exchanging happy qi with you as the two of you
explore new ways of communicating.

Coming When Called

Every cat can and should learn to come when
called. A cat call doesn't have to be limited to
"Here, kitty, kitty, kitty." Cats can easily learn
to recognize their own names. If you call "Here,
Tom" and reward Tom with a kitty delicacy, lov-

ing petting, and happy praise each time he responds to your call, soon Tom will come to you every time. By giving your cat a food reward when he responds to you, you have activated his prey drive. You appeal to his innate nature, because he likes to greet you. Coming to you when called is fun and exciting.

Coming when called can save your cat's life. Imagine if your indoor cat has slipped out the door, or if your indoor/outdoor animal companion has become disoriented because you have moved to a new house. Your cat's ability to come when called can help her find the safety of her home.

Speak

Speaking on cue also can save your cat's life. She could be lost outside but too nervous to leave her hiding place to come to you. Your animal companion may become trapped in a closet or in the clothes dryer and unable to come to you when you call her. A cat who speaks on cue can lead you to her.

When you know that your cat is about to meow, say "Speak." Give her a treat for speaking. Repeat this process a few times, and soon you will have a cat who reliably speaks on cue.

Sit and Down

"Sit," "down," "sit up," and similar behaviors are taught by luring the cat into position with a food reward. To teach "sit," hold a tidbit in your fingers and pull the treat back directly behind the cat's nose. She will have to put herself into a sitting position to track the treat. Say "good sit" when she does so, and give her the reward. After you have done this a few times, she will sit when you ask her to.

Teach "sit up" after the cat fully understands "sit." When the cat is sitting on cue, say "paws up" and pull the treat up a couple of inches higher. The sitting cat will straighten her spine to reach her "prey."

Teach "down" from a sit position. Take the food lure and pull it directly in front of his nose, between his front paws, and then out in front of her in an "L" shape. To capture the food "prey," the cat will automatically go into the down position. Some cats won't lie down even to follow a lure. Try laying your hand *gently* on your cat's back. Soft pressure will guide her into the down position. Anything stronger than the lightest touch will cause her to stand up as an opposition reflex.

Naturally Occurring Behaviors

Your cat can learn to do any naturally occurring behavior on cue. For example, many cats wave. When your cat waves, say "Good wave" and give her a food treat. Watch for behaviors that are fun for your cat and teach her a cue word for those actions.

I have just started training Mews, but she already comes when called, sits on cue, jumps wherever I ask her, and does "paws up." She is now in the process of learning to lie down on cue and to wave. She purrs loudly every time we play our training games, obviously hugely enjoying these sessions with her favorite human.

Cats who learn these exercises have an improved relationship with their human companions. Since your cat will receive a food reward every time she does what you ask, training is an amusing game to your cat that allows her to use her clever mind. Your cat feels the joyful exchange of qi every time she does what you ask her to. What could be better from a cat's perspective?

Training will benefit other areas of your cat's life as well. For example, she will be calmer when being examined by a veterinarian, because you have spent so much time handling her.

PART FOUR

Restoring
the Balance

CATS OUT OF BALANCE

Perhaps because cats are naturally in such perfect harmony with the world around them, when things go wrong with a cat they can go horribly wrong. Cats can destroy furniture, urinate all over a home, and mutilate themselves.

You can help your cat to come back to the right balance in his life. He may need for you to help him regain a sense of calm in his own territory. He may need you to help him regain his stillness.

Although many behavior problems indicate a cat who needs help and support, other misdeeds are problems only from a human perspective. They are perfectly normal behaviors to a cat.

Many of the problems that humans experience with their feline companions stem from the innate natures of both humans and cats: We are both very territorial creatures. We come into conflict when a cat wants to tear into his furniture with his claws, while we want to invite friends over to admire the same furniture.

It seems normal to us when humans mark their territories with the scent of soap or perfume; it is upsetting to us when cats mark the territory with the scent of urine. Fortunately, there are ways that we can live harmoniously and solve these problems to the satisfaction of both human and feline household members.

This section explores common behavior problems and methods for treating those problems. The solutions to your cat's behavior problems are all nonviolent. They are also effective, because they respond to the problem with an understanding of the behavior from your cat's perspective.

All of the solutions are based on the Taoist principles that have been discussed in this book. Each solution addresses how your meditative sense of stillness, your understanding of your cat's innate nature, the exchange of qi with your cat, and the principle of wu wei can help you to solve the problem. By focusing on the precepts of Taoism, you can give your cat practical help.

Practical Application of the Tao: Destructive Scratching

Anyone who lives with a cat knows that cats scratch things. Unfortunately, sometimes a cat destroys objects that are important to the humans in the household.

The Unenlightened Response

Many people respond to this damage by yelling at the cat or squirting him with a water bottle every time the cat goes near the furniture. This solution isn't effective, of course, because the cat will still scratch the furniture whenever the humans leave the house. The yelling and water squirting only reduce the level of love and trust—the exchange of qi—from the cat.

Some people take the drastic step of declawing their cats, since they don't like constantly confronting the scratching problem. Declawing leaves the cat mutilated and unable to protect himself from danger.

There are better solutions.

The Problem from the Cat's Perspective

Cats physically need to scratch. It sloughs off old layers of nails and sharpens their claws. Cats also are claiming territory when they scratch at surfaces. In addition, the motion of scratching is important exercise for your cat's paws, forelegs, shoulders, and back. The movement energizes the flow of qi through the cat's body.

The goal is to transfer your cat's desire to scratch on your furniture, wallpaper, or antique Persian rug and redirect his energy to his scratching posts. This is done by making your scratching posts more appealing than your furniture or other forbidden objects.

Different cats like to scratch different surfaces. In addition to traditional carpet-covered scratching posts, offer your cat posts covered with sisal, natural wood, or cardboard. Giving your cat a choice of materials does not have to be expensive. Cardboard scratching posts infused with catnip are available at many pet supply stores. You also can make your own scratching posts for just a few dollars.

It is important that your cat's scratching posts are built tall enough to let your animal companion fully stretch out his body. (That full-body stretch is one of his cat qigong forms.) Also give your cat some horizontal scratching surfaces, since many cats like to scratch at something on the ground. Posts must have a solid, strong base, because a cat won't use one that tips or wobbles when he tries to scratch it.

Many people rake their cat's paws against a scratching post to try to get the cat interested in it. That is a mistake, since it is an attempt to force a cat into an action. Force, no matter how well intended, never achieves results with a cat. The cat usually will respond by avoiding the scratching post.

To get your cat to try the post, cover the post with catnip and run a string or feather along the surface. As your cat pounces on the toy, he'll discover that he likes the sensation of sinking his claws into his new post. From that time on, he will enjoy his post.

At the same time you make your cat's posts more appealing from a cat's perspective, you need to make your furniture or other forbidden scratching surface less appealing. Obviously your cat likes the feel of the furniture as he claws at it. Changing the surface to an unpleasant one will make him avoid it. This can be as simple as draping an attractive throw over the chair. The chair will no longer have the firm, immobile surface the cat had enjoyed scratching. Other deterrents include two-sided tape or aluminum foil.

Place the scratching post right next to the furniture, so when the cat scratches the post, he is still signaling that the furniture belongs to him. This satisfies his need to claim his territory.

Application of Taoist Principles in Ending Destructive Scratching

Stillness

You avoided confrontation and shouting. You were able to maintain a still, calm household. This stillness will make your cat feel safe to explore new games and toys, making use of new scratching posts more likely.

The Innate Nature of the Cat

You respected the innate nature of your cat and his need to scratch. You gave him surfaces that met his need and still met your need to have a home that isn't torn into small bits by cat claws.

Exchange of Qi

Instead of allowing the scratching to deteriorate your exchange of qi with your cat, you provided an alternative. Your cat will welcome his new posts and will enjoy playing games with you around them. Your relationship with each other will improve as a result of this solution.

Wu Wei

It is easier and more effective to deal with the furniture and the scratching posts than it is to try to change cat behavior through force or intimidation.

Practical Application of the Tao: Soiling in the House

From a cat's perspective, there are two kinds of house soiling. One is failure to use the litter box for urination and defecation. The other is territorial marking. This section deals with failure to use the litter box. The next one covers territorial marking.

The Unenlightened Response

People are extremely emotional about a cat's failure to use the litter box. Although part of the conflict comes from the unpleasantness of cleaning up cat waste, a larger part of the human frustration comes from our own innate natures. The cat soiling in the house has violated our sense of territory in our homes. Responses to house soiling are therefore often irrational and cruel. It does no good at all to rub a cat's nose in the accident or to hit him for the mistake. Cats have reasons for making these housebreaking mistakes, and simple, nonviolent solutions to the problem exist.

Use of a litter box is an amazing thing. House-training all other domestic creatures (especially humans) takes a lot of time and effort. While people and other creatures can learn to be clean, they don't come by it automatically. However, almost every cat, even those who were orphaned, figures out how to use a kitty litter box. It is a testament to the clean nature of this creature that he looks at a box of sand or clay in the laundry room and figures out that it is the best place for his toilet needs.

Still, sometimes there are problems and cats decide that the litter box is not the best place to urinate and defecate. Fortunately, by looking at the problem from the cat's perspective, there are often solutions to this problem.

The Problem from the Cat's Perspective

Cats, who are by nature very clean and private creatures, are being asked to use a litter box for their intimate bodily functions. A cat may find a litter box unacceptable for a number of different reasons. The following is a list of the most common reasons that a cat rejects a litter box, followed by the solution to the problem.

Rejection Reason #1

The cat has a urinary tract infection or other physical problem that makes bladder or bowel control difficult.

Solution

The first step in any litter box problem is always to take the cat to a veterinarian for a thorough physical examination. Once the cat's physical problem is cured, his house soiling problem also will be cured.

Rejection Reason #2

Cats may refuse to use a litter box that isn't cleaned often enough. Although some cats will endure filthy boxes, others don't want a trace of waste in them. Just because a box seems to be clean to our inadequate human noses does not mean that it is not noxious to a highly developed feline olfactory system.

Solution

Clean the litter box every time the cat uses it. If you are not home often enough to do this, provide extra litter boxes for the cat or experiment with the new models that clean up automatically after a cat uses them.

Rejection Reason #3

In multiple-cat households, some cats won't share litter boxes.

Solution

Provide one litter box per cat if you are having problems.

Rejection Reason #4

In Nature, most cats urinate and defecate in different areas. Some cats will not urinate and defecate in the same box.

Solution

Give your cat two litter boxes if you find that he is using his current box for just one bodily function.

Rejection Reason #5

Different cats prefer different styles of litter. Many don't like the sharp particles in traditional litter. Others don't like scented litter. Some cats were taught to use soil by their outdoor cat mother and don't realize that you want them to use a litter box filled with a commercial product.

Solution

If possible, use the same kind of litter that your cat had as a kitten. If you adopt a cat from a shelter or pick up a stray, offer a couple of different kinds of litter at first to see what the cat prefers. If your cat wants to use a substance that is very inconvenient or makes you feel your home is unsanitary, you can change him over — gradually. For example, if your cat wants to use soil and you want to use a commercial product, add a small amount of the product to the soil daily, so that after a month or two, you have changed your cat over to the new product.

Rejection Reason #6

Cats want a private, but not necessarily enclosed, litter box. Many cats will refuse to use boxes with covers or boxes that are in the middle of high-traffic areas in the household.

Solution

Think about the box from your cat's point of view. If the box is covered and he is refusing to use it, remove the cover and see if he does better. Think about the location of the box: Is it someplace that denies him the privacy your cat may need?

Rejection Reason #7

For unaccountable reasons, your cat may prefer a different location for his toilet.

Solution

If your cat consistently uses a spot other than his litter box, consider placing his box in the location that he likes to use. If that is not possible (it is reasonable for humans to prefer the litter box not be placed by the dining room table or next to the bed), make the place the cat has been using unappealing. Cover the spot with aluminum foil or plastic, surfaces that are not pleasant for toilets. Place his food on top of the plastic or foil; a cat will not defecate or urinate in the spot where he eats.

Rejection Reason #8

The cat has become disoriented and is not following his regular toilet habits. You tried all of the previous suggestions but they did not work.

Solution

You may need to rehousebreak your cat. Confine your animal companion to a small room, preferably one with a surface that is easy to clean. Place all his food, water, bed, and favorite toys in the room on the opposite side from the kitty litter box. Anytime the cat uses the litter box in your presence, praise him, pet him, and give him treats. (Be sure to visit with him in the room several times a day. You are trying to solve his house soiling problem, not punishing him.)

After your cat has used the litter box in this confined space perfectly for at least five days, expand his territory into a second room. Keep him confined to that room for a few days. If that succeeds, gradually add one room at a time to your cat's territory.

Application of Taoist Principles in Solving Litter Box Problems

Stillness

Your cat is concerned and upset, since urinating or defecating outside his litter box is against his natural instincts to be clean. Yelling at the cat, hitting him, or rubbing his nose in the waste would almost certainly have made the problem worse. A calm, quiet response helps to reassure the cat and resolves the problem most quickly.

The Innate Nature of the Cat

You relied on your cat's innate sense of cleanliness. You just had to learn how the cat views his need to be clean rather than relying on your perception of cleanliness.

Exchange of Qi

You praised and rewarded your cat for using the litter box. By solving the problem, you eliminated a source of frustration that was reducing the exchange of qi between you.

Wu Wei

By acknowledging your cat's needs, you were able to solve a problem that would be unsolvable otherwise.

Practical Application of the Tao: Territorial Marking

Cats urinate to establish territory. It is surprising to humans that a cat who will carefully cover his urine in the box will then turn around and spray the wall next to the box. Understanding that this is territorial behavior rather than a housebreaking problem will help to redirect the behavior more quickly.

Spraying is most common in unneutered males (most of them spray at least occasionally) and least common in spayed females (about 5 percent spray).

The Problem from the Cat's Perspective

Cats spray to tell other cats about their sexual availability and to announce that a territory belongs to them. When you understand why your cat is spraying, you can solve the problem.

Spraying Reason #1

The cat is an intact male or female, announcing his or her sexual availability.

Solution

If you are having a spraying problem with an unaltered cat, spaying or neutering the cat will drastically reduce the likelihood of this behavior.

Spraying Reason #2

You have made changes in your life that are disruptive to your cat, so he is spraying to reassure himself and others that the territory still belongs to him.

Solution

Try to eliminate the cause of your cat's stress. If that's not possible, help your cat associate these changes with good things from you. For example, if the cause of stress is the arrival of a new roommate, feed, stroke, play, and talk to your animal companion in the presence of your new roommate. Let the cat know that his life is better, not worse, as a result of the change in the household.

Spraying Reason #3

Once a critical mass of cats has been reached, spraying is inevitable. Cats who live in too close proximity to other cats have a biological need to mark the territory.

Solution

If spraying is caused by the fact that you have too many cats in the household, it is a good idea to find loving homes for one or more of your cats. Although cats are much more social than most people realize, they do not do well in large numbers in small areas.

Spraying is a sign of their stress. Cats kept in close proximity to other cats live shorter, less healthy lives than other cats. How many cats are too many depends on the personalities of the cats involved, the nature of the space, and the personal history of the cats.

Spraying Reason #4

Some cats have a high level of territorial urge and will continue to spray even after being neutered and living in a tranquil environment.

Solution

There are two solutions to consider for this cat. One is attempting to rehousebreak the cat by confining him in one room, as was described in the "Soiling in the House" section. Your cat is feeling out of control in his current territory. Shrinking that territory to a small, controlled space may free him from the need to mark the room. Once he is calm and has stopped spraying in this space for at least five days, gradually add to his territory as long as he does not resume his marking behavior.

The second solution is a new product that has come on the market called Feliway. It is available through veterinarians. Simply spritz a small amount of the product on any area the cat tends to spray. Feliway replicates the cat's facial scent. Since cats will almost never spray a surface with urine that they mark with their face, your cat shouldn't spray urine on a surface that's been treated with Feliway. According to product studies, urine spraying is almost completely eliminated within two weeks.

Application of Taoist Principles in Solving Territorial Marking

Stillness

Yelling at the cat would have worsened the problem, making him feel more insecure. Territorial marking indicates that the cat is feeling insecure in his environment.

The Innate Nature of the Cat

Cats have an innate need to mark their territories, especially in times of stress. Most of the solutions listed eliminated either the urge to spray or the cause of the spraying. Use of

Feliway replicates the cat's clean nature, which dictates that he not rub his face in a place that he marks with urine.

Exchange of Qi

Your cat is feeling insecure in his territory and is marking to strengthen his hold in your house. When he feels this level of tension, his relationship with you is deteriorating. Solving the problem will improve your relationship and the flow of qi between you.

Wu Wei

There is no benefit to struggling with the cat. Dealing with the root of the problem is easier and more effective.

Practical Application of the Tao: Moving a Cat to a New Home

Cats, we know, are the most territorial of creatures. On their own, few cats would decide to pack up and move across the country. They are almost always nervous, and usually fearful, when they move into a new home. Cats frequently run away from new homes. Other cats mark territory, become aggressive, or become extremely shy and reclusive. Once you understand the nature of your cat, you can make these kinds of transitions much easier for him.

The Problem from the Cat's Perspective

Because cats are extremely territorial beings, being on unfamiliar ground feels dangerous. Frightened cats will either try to escape back to their old territories or hide in a small space to assess the new situation.

Solution

Confine your animal companion to a single room when you first move into a new home. Preferably, the room should be easy to clean and have noncarpeted floors, since your cat may spray to establish his territory. Place his litter box at one end of the room and his food, water, and familiar toys at the other. Sprinkle catnip on his scratching post, bed, and toys.

Visit with your cat in his room many times each day, letting him know how much you love him. Tell him how much he will learn to enjoy his new home. Groom and pet him as much as he will welcome.

This confinement is not cruel. It replicates the way a cat moves into a new territory naturally. A cat will pick a small, secure area in which to hide while he evaluates the new place. Unfortunately, the "safe" place he may choose could be under your car or in the washing machine. By confining your cat to a single room, you are working with his innate nature and protecting him from the very real dangers of the human world.

Keep the cat confined in the room until he fully relaxes, which usually takes about a week. Gradually add one room at a time to his territory until he has the run of the entire house.

I recently moved to a new home with my cat, Mews. We followed all the steps I've outlined. I confined her in my new bedroom, so that she would be with me all night as well as during my many daily visits with her. On the third day after we moved, she started meowing insistently, telling me she was ready to come out. I opened the door to let her into the hall. She happily stomped around the interior perimeter of the house twice, settled onto her favorite place on the couch, and began to purr. Providing her with the safety of one room to work through the move helped her adjust. She also made it clear to me when she was ready to explore.

If your cat was an outdoor cat or an indoor/outdoor cat at your old home, do not let him go outside until he's totally calm and playful in every room of the new house. This adjustment may take a month or more. If you let your animal companion outside while the house is still a strange and frightening place to him, he is likely to wander off. If you have been thinking about switching your cat to become an indoors-only cat, this is a good time to do it.

Application of Taoist Principles in Moving Your Cat to a New Home

Stillness

No matter how insecure you may feel regarding the move, it is important not to transmit those feelings to your cat. He needs your quiet assurance that all will be well.

The Innate Nature of the Cat

Although it may seem unnatural to confine the cat to a single room when he first moves, doing so replicates the way a cat in the wild moves into new territory. While he can handle a small room, he may feel overwhelmed by a whole house or a new outdoor neighborhood.

Exchange of Qi

It is very important to spend time with your cat during his confinement. You want him to feel that this is a good, happy place. He needs to learn that this will be a safe home for him through your loving words and gentle touch.

Wu Wei

It is much easier to manage a move with a cat who is safely confined to a small space. It is a terrible tragedy when cats become lost or injured because they are unfamiliar with a new territory.

Practical Application of the Tao: Multiple Cats

Cats can become fast and loving friends with other cats. In fact, households in the United States are more likely to have multiple cats than they are to have multiple dogs.

Although cats can become devoted to each other, the right introduction is very important.

The Problem from the Cat's Perspective

Until the new cat came along, the first cat had the household territory, access to food, and the attention of the human members of the household to himself. It takes most cats a period of time to decide that the friendship of another cat is worth losing some of his exclusive rights to the house.

Solution

Look for a second cat who will be compatible with your first one. As a general rule, an established cat will accept a kitten better than he will an adult. Most cats prefer to live with a member of the opposite sex. Adult cats and members of the same sex can be introduced successfully, but the process may take longer.

If possible, "introduce" the cats before bringing the new cat home. Rub the new cat with a washcloth, paying special attention to the scent glands around his ears and the corners of his mouth. Take the washcloth home and place it in your first cat's bed or use it as a placemat for his food dish. Also rub the first cat's scent onto a washcloth for the new cat. When you bring the new cat home, the two cats will already have good feelings about each other's scent.

Confine the new cat to a room, just as you did when you originally moved in with your first cat.

This time of confinement allows your new cat to adjust to your home and allows the first cat time to become accustomed to the presence of a second cat in the house. Every few days take the new cat to another room and start the process all over again.

During this time, pay extra attention to your first cat. Problems usually develop when the first cat feels jealous of the time and attention the new cat is receiving.

Soon you'll see soft paws reaching under the door to play with each other. Let your cats begin to spend small periods of time together in the same room. If that goes well, extend those periods of time. Keep the cats separated when you are away from home or while you are asleep until you are sure they are getting along well. Trim both cats' nails before they meet so no one can get hurt if they are initially less than enthused by the other's company.

Make sure you have enough toys, special places to rest, cat "condos" for climbing and sleeping, and other items that cats like. Disagreements between cats often occur when there is only one prime place to sleep or only a couple of entertaining toys.

Application of Taoist Principles in Adding a Second Cat

Stillness

The cats will sense any tension you might feel. Your serenity during this process will reassure both cats that this relationship will be beneficial for everyone.

The Innate Nature of the Cat

Cats can be friends, but they are cautious about encroachment into their territory. The process outlined here respects that caution.

Exchange of Qi

Your first cat needs your reassurance that he is not being usurped by the newcomer; instead, his life will be even better. Your second cat needs your reassurance that he is in a safe place and you won't let him be harmed by the first cat or anything or anyone else in his new home.

Wu Wei

Controlling the interaction between the cats through a closed door is much easier than controlling the interaction of two strange cats meeting face-to-face.

Practical Application of the Tao: Aggression

There is nothing that destroys the flow of qi between a human and a cat more than the cat biting or scratching a loving human. We feel emotionally wounded just as much as we feel physically wounded.

The Unenlightened Response

When a cat scratches us, we are likely to hit back. When a cat hisses, most people respond by yelling. This reaction only escalates the cycle of violence.

The Problem from the Cat's Perspective

Cats do not attack randomly. We may have to look for the reason, but one is always there. Many cats have sensitive skin and can stand only a limited amount of petting or grooming. After that point has been reached, he has to find a way to tell his human that he cannot stand any more. Other cats have a strong need for privacy and will react to invasions of that privacy with anger. (The cat does not care that you just wanted to cuddle; the cat was not ready to cuddle with you.) Other cats will feel cornered and helpless, so they use their teeth and claws to get out of a situation that feels dangerous to them.

Cats can have different thresholds of tolerance at different times in their lives. For example, I was grooming Mews just a few days after we had moved. Before we moved, she was willing to let me comb through the long fur on the back of her legs. When I did the same grooming stroke shortly after we had moved, she responded by growling and hissing at me for the first (and, so far, only) time since she had come into my home. I was startled but responded by stopping the action that was upsetting to her and talking softly with her. She let me scratch her chin, and we reaffirmed our friendship. After the incident, I realized that Mews was still a little edgy in her new environment. It was too much for her to accept grooming in sensitive spots while she was still a little uncertain about her new home. Within a couple of days she was perfectly willing to let me groom the back of her legs again.

Solution

Observe your cat carefully. Watch for the triggers of his violent behavior. Is it touching a certain part of his body? Is it petting him for a certain length of time? Is it approaching a place that he considers to be his territory?

Rarely, if ever, does a cat lash out with no warning. However, his warning may be subtle. His ears may go back on his head, or they may merely flick back and forth. His muscles may tense. You might notice some little twitches in the muscles of his back. His pupils may dilate. Learn and respect your cat's individual warning signs.

Over time, gradually desensitize your cat to the trigger of his aggression. If he reacts when you come within a foot of his bed, spend time two feet away, talking softly, making no direct eye contact. Let him see that you are no threat. Then do the same twenty inches away, and then eighteen, then at sixteen, and so on. Eventually your cat's need to respond with aggression will be reduced because he will grow accustomed to your closeness. That proximity to you will no longer trigger his aggression.

Redirected Aggression

Cats frequently redirect their aggression. For example, a cat may see a strange dog outside the window. He cannot reach the dog, but his adrenaline reaches a fever pitch. Therefore, he may turn around and attack his human or feline friend who happens to be near.

Solution

The best solution for redirected aggression is to eliminate the source of stimulation. For example, if a stray cat is outside the window, close the blinds. If the sights from a particular window often create an aggressive response in your cat, it will be to everyone's benefit to make that windowsill or that room off-limits for the cat.

A spritz of water can be a good tool to bring the cat out of his "spell." However, spraying cats with water is often overused as a method for dealing with cat behavior problems. If you are running around the house chasing your cat with a water bottle, you are misusing the tool. To the cat, you are acting like an aggressive, frightening predator. A spray of water or a quick clap of your hands should merely be a distraction to bring the cat away from his destructive behavior.

Thus, if your cat is stimulated by a cat outside and redirects the aggression toward another cat in your house, a quick spritz of water can make your cat come back into the present. Often he will end his aggression. The spritz of water, used in this manner, is not punishment; it is a distraction.

Application of Taoist Principles in Reducing Aggression

Stillness

You have to respond to the aggression with internal stillness. In most cases, the best response is to take a step away from the cat and give him the space that he needs.

The Innate Nature of the Cat

Your cat will use his claws and teeth when he feels cornered, hurt, or frightened. You must respect why the cat is acting aggressively.

Exchange of Qi

Your cat will give you warning signs. Respect them. By gradually working to desensitize your cat to whatever bothers him, you will be developing a stronger bond and exchange of qi over time.

Wu Wei

Dealing with the root causes of your cat's aggressive behavior slowly erodes the problem, just as the stream erodes the boulder. Change that occurs in small increments is the most permanent kind of change.

12

CRACKS IN THE UNCARVED BLOCK
Excesses and Extremes

In Taoism, uncarved wood is considered to be the thing of most perfect beauty. When humans try to "improve" a block of wood by carving it, we only ruin what Nature has already made perfect. The more we intervene with the perfection of Nature, the farther we are from the Tao.

There is no more perfectly formed creature than a cat. Her eyes are ideally suited to day and night hunting. Her mobile ears pick up noise from vast distances. Her whiskers sense the tiniest vibrations. She has a keen sense of smell. She is an acrobat. Cats typify the Taoist ideal of the Uncarved Block.

Until recently, cats have been nearly exempt from humans' meddlesome tampering. Even with the advent of cat shows a hundred years ago, there were few extremes. Longhaired cats were developed into breed types. Animals with specific markings, such as Siamese and Birmans, were standardized. Still, cats retained the basic functional body type that nature had decreed for thousands of years.

Then humans got more sophisticated. Vanity and a desire to prove just how far humans can manipulate genes has become the rage at cat shows. "Extreme" Persians rule at shows, with faces so flat that they often have severe difficulty breathing. Many require surgery to widen their nostrils so they can breathe freely. Their eyes water because of the unnatural conformation of their faces. Now "Peke-faced" Persians have arrived. These cats have noses so flat that they are actually indented on the animal's face. "Peke-faced" and "extreme" Persians often must give birth by cesarean section because of the kittens' large, broad, flat faces.

But extremism doesn't end with Persians. These days any cat with a genetic mutation is declared to be a new breed. At least one hundred years ago tailless Manx cats were introduced. What most people don't know is that when a tailless Manx is bred to another tailless Manx, a fourth of the kittens die in the womb at an early stage of development. Even when a cat with a tail and a tailless cat mate, there is a higher incidence of stillbirths, early deaths, and spinal deformities than in other cats.

Scottish Folds are descended from a cat named Susie who was noticed in 1961. These cats have ears that fold down instead of standing erect. Like the Manx cats, it is lethal to breed a folded-eared cat to another folded-eared cat. In these fold-to-fold breedings, a quarter of the kittens will be born with osteodystrophy, a potentially deadly bone malformation.

Siamese and related "exotic" cats have been bred to be bizarrely skinny and angular. These cats exhibit none of the soft yin roundness of the normal cat. To create such extremes, cats commonly are inbred to set type. Inbred cats have a far higher risk of genetic defects than cats who are bred to unrelated mates.

The Book of Chuang Tzu warns us:

One on the true path does not lose his
    innate given nature.
To such a man that which is united
    presents no problem;
That which is divided is all right;
What is long is not too long;
That which is short is not too short.
The duck's legs for example are short,

but trying to lengthen them would
cause pain.
The legs of a crane are long, but trying to
shorten them would produce grief.
That which nature makes long we should
not cut,
Nor should we stretch what nature makes
short.
That would not solve anything.[1]

The development of unhealthy, unnatural cats
is certainly against the principles of Taoism and
is the antithesis of what is good and right for our
cats. No matter what we do to artificially change
a cat's exterior through extreme breeding prac-
tices, the creature below the skin still carries the
nature of a cat. He longs to be able to play,
jump, run, and climb. It is unfair to a cat to
create a body that does not allow him to live
within his innate nature.

Practical Application of the Tao: Finding a Cat Without Excesses and Extremes

Most of us look for our cats at the local animal shelter. This is an exceptionally good place to find a cat. Not only will you be saving a life, you will have a large selection of natural cats. If you like purebred cats, surprising numbers of them can be found at shelters throughout the nation.

If you decide to purchase a purebred cat from a breeder, look carefully at what you are buying. Fortunately, although extreme types of cats are popular at cat shows, they have not caught on with the general public. It is certainly possible to find a purebred cat that is mentally and physically sound.

Look at the nostrils of a Persian or Himalayan cat to see if there is enough of an opening to allow a free flow of air. Tell the breeders you prefer the "dollface" type (with a small nose) to the "extreme" or "Peke-faced" type (with little or no length to the nose).

Look carefully at the bone development of Manx cats and Scottish Folds. Feel any cat you may bring home for a sound, healthy body type.

Every kitten is adorable. Look at the kitten's parents. Do they have a natural, healthy look to them?

A purebred kitten should have a pedigree that lists all his ancestors for at least three generations. Ask to look at the kitten's pedigree in order to avoid purchasing an inbred cat with the concomitant higher incidence of genetic problems. (If you see a breeding pattern on the cat's pedigree that would be illegal for humans in your state, look for another kitten.)

A Word to Cat Breeders

If you are thinking about breeding purebred cats, become knowledgeable about the genetic problems faced by the breed. If you do not follow the proper protocols for mating Manx cats or Scottish Folds, you are condemning kittens to preventable misery. For every kitten you bring into the world, you should ask yourself if this will be a healthy, balanced cat who can expect to enjoy a long, active life. If the answer is not an unqualified yes, then the litter should never be bred.

If only unhealthy specimens of a breed win at cat shows, it is time to rethink the hobby. Some organizations seem to be pulling back from the brink of extremism in cats. What joy can a human feel when the animal who wins at a show is unable to breathe well and is built in a manner that requires a cesarean section to bear young?

Lao Tzu said, "The Sage rejects the extreme, the excessive, and the extravagant."[2] So should every cat breeder.

Too Many Cats

Nature, in its eternal way, limits the number of cougars, lions, and other cats in the wild. If there is not enough food, cats starve. When adults are out hunting, other predators take their young.

We have no natural balance in our urban world. Even feral cats generally have enough food to be able to reproduce, although their kittens are consigned to a short, hard life of deprivation and disease. Cats raised as indoor companions are prolific. A female cat can have more than a hundred babies in her lifetime. And each female baby can have a hundred babies.

The de facto method of dealing with all these cats is massive euthanasia. Most of these deaths take place at animal shelters, where, typically, sad and dedicated workers euthanize three-quarters of the cats who come through the door.

Feral cats, living in the shadow of disease and starvation, may be less fortunate than the shelter cats, who at least have a quick death. Then there are the countless cats who die slowly of starvation, because their humans dumped them off at a forest, farm, or park, assuming the cat or kitten would somehow fend for herself.

The only solution to this annual massacre of millions of unwanted cats is to spay or neuter your cat. For those who question whether this is truly a natural, Taoist solution, I can only answer that spaying and neutering are the only ways cats can lead happy Taoist lives without contributing to the overpopulation problem.

There is a growing movement to spay and neuter feral cats. Volunteer groups catch cats in humane traps, spay or neuter the animals, then release them back to their neighborhoods. The feral cats live longer, healthier lives when they can focus their energies on eating and fending for themselves rather than on mating, fighting, or raising kittens.

Taoism reveres long, healthy lives. In order for cats to enjoy long lives, we must spay and neuter far more than we do today.

Declawing

Cats have claws for more reasons than just scratching your furniture. Their claws are part of their balance. Claws help cats catch prey, whether the prey is a mouse or a string that is pulled across the floor. Claws are a part of the balance of soft and hard, yin and yang, that is intrinsic to the cat's nature. Cats give and receive an energy flow through their claws.

Declawing is an unnatural and unnecessary intervention with your cat's body. If your cat scratches objects that you would prefer she does not, work with her to direct her normal scratching behavior in constructive ways. Don't amputate her toes.

There is a significant difference between spaying and neutering a cat (arguably an unnatural operation) and declawing a cat. If cats are not spayed and neutered, their offspring or the offspring of other cats face certain death. Spaying and neutering save cats' lives. Declawing is for the benefit of humans and their possessions, not for the benefit of the cat.

Wild Cats

Wild cats belong in the wild. It is inexpressibly sad to read of someone who keeps a tiger or a mountain lion in a cage because he or she "loves wild cats." People who love these magnificent animals should let them live free.

Occasionally people try to breed domestic cats with wild ones. This is not the Tao of either creature. Domestic cats are intrinsically different from wild creatures. For thousands of years, they have chosen to join us in our homes and on our farms.

Millions of cats are euthanized in shelters every year. People who say they love cats should let the tiger live in the jungle and save the life of a cat who needs a human to love.

The Resiliency of the Uncarved Block

Although the world is a far from perfect place for our feline companions, it is a better place than it was in the past. Although millions of cats still are being slaughtered for want of a home, the numbers are half what they were twenty years ago.

More people are providing loving, responsible care for their cats. When I was a child, my family provided our dogs with vaccinations and other preventive veterinary care. Our cats received only emergency medical attention, and undoubtedly they had better care than most cats in the neighborhood. That neglect would be unthinkable to anyone I know, including my family members, today. These days cats are living longer, healthier lives.

Declawing is also falling out of favor. Many people I know who declawed previous cats have allowed their current animal companions to keep their claws. Today the operation is not undertaken so lightly.

Although cat show exhibitors are evolving ever more bizarre versions of their favorite breeds, the general public has shown little interest in the exaggerated cats that are produced. Most still seek a cat with centuries-old features that combine soft and hard, sleek and round, tough and sweet.

So, the cat, resilient predator, is proving to be a resilient friend in our hearts and homes. That is as it should be.

13

HEALTHY LIVING
Protecting Your Cat's Immune System

Taoists have a reverence for natural health. The daily attacks on your cat's immune system—pollution in the air, noise and chaos of the city, and emotional stress in a household—all contribute to health problems in cats.

Your cat has enough unhealthy physical and emotional influences to process. Do not add to that burden by giving him food that is laced with preservatives, additives, artificial colors, and artificial flavors. Fortunately, there are an array of healthful choices available for your cat.

Cooking for Your Cat

Increasing numbers of people are cooking for their cats. This is not a process to be taken lightly, since a cat's nutritional requirements are significantly different from a human's. For example, it is absolutely essential that a cat's diet include taurine. A vegetarian diet, unless it has extensive and correct supplementation, will make your cat extremely ill.

If you are interested in learning how to cook properly for your cat, a number of books are available through Direct Book Service's extensive *Dog and Cat Book Catalogue* (1-800-776-2665; www.dogandcatbooks.com).

Prepackaged Foods

Many pet supply stores offer a wide variety of "natural" cat foods. Since there are no regulatory guidelines on what "natural" means, read the labels carefully. Try to avoid any products that contain the chemical preservatives BHA, BHT, or ethoxyquin. Foods can be preserved with vitamin C or vitamin E instead, and are much healthier that way.

Look for the quality of ingredients on the labels. By-products may not have the same absorbable nutrition that animal meat has. "Animals are healthier eating beef than beaks," says one person.

Vitamins

After decades of skepticism, the medical community has concluded that a daily vitamin supplement keeps humans healthier. It is common sense that a vitamin supplement correctly formulated for a cat's unique nutritional needs will keep our cats healthier as well. The right vitamin supplements, taken in the proper amounts, can even help rebuild the immune system of animals whose systems have been compromised (such as cats with allergies, cancer, or arthritis).

Flea Products

For decades, we have covered our cats with incredibly toxic chemicals in order to stave off flea
infestations. Many cats have died as a result.

I will never forget the last day I used insecti-
cides to kill fleas. I had brought home a dog who
had fleas. The condominium I lived in became
infested. Carefully following the directions of
the flea products that I had purchased from my
veterinarian, I gave my dog a flea bath; took my
cat, Silver Lining, to the groomer for a flea bath;
and "flea bombed" the condo. Even at that time
in my life, I was concerned about all the chemicals and made sure that my home was aired out
for an extra-long period of time before the animals were allowed inside.

The next morning Silver Lining was sitting on
the couch next to me and suddenly fell off. She
went into seizures. Since it was a Sunday, I
rushed Silver Lining to the emergency veterinary clinic. The verdict: The flea treatments had
caused the seizures. The veterinarian at the
emergency clinic said that it was not unusual to

see this kind of problem. We were very lucky that the seizures ended after a few minutes. The episode left no overt health problems, but it scared me enough that I resolved never to use products like those again.

Many all-natural, nontoxic flea treatment alternatives exist. If a severe infestation will not respond to products such as pennyroyal, eucalyptus, or diatomaceous earth, new products such as Advantage, while still posing some risk, are much safer than the old flea powders, baths, collars, and bombs.

Resources

An increasing number of stores around the country specialize in all-natural products. One of the first, and still one of the best, is the Holistic Pet Center, 15599 S.E. 82nd Drive, Clackamas, OR 97015. Their catalog of all-natural foods, vitamins, flea remedies, and other products is available by calling 1-800-788-PETS (7387). Not only are their products first rate, their staff is highly knowledgeable and very concerned about animals' well-being.

Complementary Medicine

Traditional Chinese medicine, which is in concert with Taoist principles, has existed for at least four thousand years. *The Yellow Emperor's Classic of Medicine* was possibly the first medical text of all time. It delineates how to achieve good health and long life by following the Tao, balancing yin and yang, and responding to the four seasons.

Acupuncture reflects a Taoist understanding of the universe and human bodies. Disciplines such as naturopathy and chiropractic are strongly influenced by traditional Chinese medicine and its goal of restoring a body to its natural balance. My acupuncturist likes to point out that the Chinese consider Western medicine to be "experimental."

Throughout the world, veterinarians are turning to alternative medicine as well. This can be very important for the treatment of our cats, since their systems have much more trouble dealing with drugs than do humans or other animals, such as dogs. In fact, even aspirin can be lethal to a cat.

Alternative veterinary medicine is still in its infancy. My acupuncturist attended a three-year postcollege course in order to be considered for a license to practice in the state of Oregon. My chiropractor and naturopath also had to complete years of graduate education and pass competency examinations. However, any veterinarian can call himself or herself a "holistic veterinarian" and practice without any substantive knowledge in the field. Some who practice are truly excellent and can do your cat a great deal of good. Others raise some cause for concern.

When looking for an alternative veterinary medical practitioner, a good place to start is with the American Holistic Veterinary Medical Association, which can be reached at 410-569-0795, and the International Veterinary Acupuncture Society, at 303-682-1167. These associations sponsor courses and seminars to provide high-quality information to their members.

If you or someone you know goes to an acupuncturist, naturopath, or other alternative health provider, these practitioners may be able to suggest a competent holistic veterinarian. There is a good chance that your acupuncturist has sought out alternative medical care for his or her animal companions.

Finally, trust your own judgment. No one knows your cat better than you do. If the alternative veterinary medical practitioner's suggestions seem to make sense to you, follow them. Doing so can make a big difference in your cat's quality of life.

Healthy Aging

Growing old is a natural part of our lives. However, Western culture tries to deny the aging process. We seem to search endlessly for the Fountain of Youth.

Taoists (and the Chinese culture in general)

revere the benefits of a long, healthy life. Instead of trying to escape from the reality of aging, age is embraced.

It will help your animal companion's well-being in her older years if you embrace a Taoist view of age.

Your Aging Cat

There is something incredibly satisfying about being in the presence of an old cat. The years have diminished the cat's fiery, airy yang energy, leaving her with the solidness of the earth. Many old cats have a relaxation to their muscles that feels good to our touch. Their hours of sleep and rest increase, and they make perfect companions on long, cold nights.

Revel in the beauty of your old cat. She may not have the sleekness of her youth, but she has a dignity that comes only from years of life. Her character is set in her eyes and the way she walks. Aging is not to be mourned, for your cat's best years may be the ones in which she rests and relaxes in the quietness of her home.

In the West, when we think of age we think of death. Instead, enjoy this time in your companion's life and relish the old friend who purrs in your arms.

Although old age is not to be feared, it is important not to forget the physical wear that age brings to your cat. There is much you can do to help your cat to feel more comfortable and even live longer.

Alleviating the Pain of Arthritis

Almost every elderly cat develops arthritis. The years of jumping and landing take their toll on your animal companion's leg joints and spine. Western medicine has few answers for arthritic cats. Aspirin and related products are very toxic to cats, so there is little pain relief available. Fortunately, there is a growing field of complementary medical treatments available to help your cat.

Nutraceuticals

A variety of natural products can assist your cat's body to replenish joint cartilage. Most of these products contain glucosamine. These nutraceuticals have been clinically proven to reduce pain and may slow down the development of arthritis. One brand, Cosequin, is available at many veterinary offices. I gave my cat Silver Lining a brand called Arthi-Soothe for the last year of her life. She was definitely more mobile when she took this supplement.

Acupuncture

Acupuncture also can relieve the pain of arthritis. We Westerners who grew up with the pain of vaccination needles are often afraid to try acupuncture, assuming it will hurt. Yet acupuncture is not painful to cats (or to people). Needles for vaccinations are designed to tear through skin and create a hole. Acupuncture needles are designed to work their way between the layers of skin. Millions of Americans have now experienced acupuncture and have benefited from its

pain-reducing powers. Now, in many places in
the country, your cat can do the same.

Chiropractic

Just as chiropractic manipulation can reduce
pain and increase function for people with arthritis, it also can provide assistance for cats.
The American Veterinary Chiropractic Association was begun by a veterinarian who found the
tools available to her to be too limiting, so she
completed a four-year chiropractic education.
She then developed an intensive monthlong
course that teaches licensed veterinarians and licensed chiropractors how to give chiropractic
manipulation to animals. Practitioners who have
completed the American Veterinary Chiropractic Association course can provide safe manipu-
lations for your cat.

Healing Touch

Healing touch is the manipulation of the qi field
around your cat's body. Without touching your
cat, rake your fingers through the air about an

inch over her body. Bring a flow of energy from her head, down her spine, past her pelvis, down her legs, and out through her feet. Shake the old qi off your hand and repeat several times.

Although there are significant scientific data that prove the efficacy of acupuncture and chiropractic, less information is available about healing touch. However, it certainly can't hurt your cat to massage the air around her body. It might help her. I did this technique for Silver Lining, and she purred with pleasure each time we did it. At the very least, you are providing your cat with a happy experience with you. And there is reason to believe that you are actually physically helping her body to heal itself. Try it. See if your cat enjoys it as much as Silver Lining did.

Diseases of the Kidney

At some point in her older years, your cat's kidneys are almost certain to begin to lose some of their function. Your cat's body cannot keep up with the demands that her fiery yang energy places on her kidneys.

Your veterinarian probably will recommend a low-protein prescription formula for your cat. Lower protein intake will reduce the stress on the cat's kidneys. Unfortunately, most veterinarians offer prescription cat foods that are laced with preservatives. Ingredients such as BHT, BHA, and ethoxyquin are preservatives that may be difficult for your cat's liver and kidney to process.

Take the nutritional information from the label of the prescription food and find an all-natural product that provides the same levels of protein and other key ingredients. By doing so, you will be helping your cat eat properly for her kidney condition without taxing her weakened immune system with preservatives and other deleterious substances.

Kidney Healing

Your cat may benefit from a healing technique that I was once taught. Rub your hands together until your palms are warm. Then place your hands over your cat's kidneys (about two inches in front of his hipbones). Feel a flow of healing qi energy come from the air, through your palms, into your cat's kidneys.

Do not give your cat your own energy; that will just deplete you. Instead visualize energy coming from the universe, flowing through your hands and into the cat's kidneys. After holding your hands on her body for a couple of minutes, shake the old qi off. Then rake the air above your cat in the same way as described in the healing touch technique.

Once again, there is no proof that this technique helps your cat. But it can't hurt her, and she will surely enjoy the feeling of your touch. Watching Silver Lining relax and stretch out her body and purr loudly, I am certain in my own heart that it made her feel better. I am glad that I did this for her.

In my own personal medical treatments, I combine what my Western doctor has to offer with what alternative medical practitioners can do for me. I believe it is prudent and compassionate to do the same for my animal companions.

14

Peaceful Death

Even when we do everything that alternative and Western medicine can offer for our animal companions, their life spans are not infinite. Nature has designed their years on this earth to be fewer than our own. At some point, the end of life on this plane draws near.

Because we are sad at the impending loss of our friend, many humans draw away from their sick cats. After all the years of friendship that your cat has given to you, he deserves your time, love, and attention during his last months.

Talk to your old cat. Tell him stories about your life together. Remind him how thrilled you were when he came to live with you. Talk about your adventures together—the insects he's caught, the way he used to come running to tell you that he was seeing snow through the windowpane, his habit of sitting right next to anyone with a cat allergy. When you tell him these stories of his life, form vivid pictures in your mind of the events. Your cat may be able to recognize the pictures that you share.

Your old cat is less likely to initiate contact when he is not feeling entirely well, so initiate it for him. Pet him and groom him. Fuss over him and thank him for the part he has played in your life.

The Purr

Animal writers often point out how odd it is that cats purr when they are sick. These writers must have never listened to a sick cat purring.

A sick cat's purr is entirely different from the joyful crescendo of a meditating cat or the loud tones of approval he gives to his human companion during petting or feeding. The purr of a sick cat is thready and far less substantial than those happy purrs. A healthy purr is an exultation of life. A sick cat's purr is much more like a lullaby a cat sings to comfort himself.

A healthy purr helps a cat focus inward. Next time you hear a sick cat purr, you will discover it seems to focus a cat away from his body. It is a sweet, delicate distraction from the reality of his illness. Its difference from his other purrs is unmistakable.

Practical Application of the Tao: Transition from this Life

Lao Tzu said:

To die but not to perish is to be eternally present.[1]

Taoism provides a reassuring, even positive, perspective on the cycle of death and birth.

We are all part of the Tao. All creatures were connected to the Tao before we were in our current physical bodies, and we will be connected to it after we leave these bodies. Our spirits existed as part of the Tao before we took the physical body we have in this life; when we die we free ourselves of our bodily form and return to the Tao from which we came.

Like the eternal cycle of the seasons, there is nothing sad or wrong with the cycles of our lives. However you personally envision the next phase of being, Taoist philosophy is clear that our death is no more to be mourned than the beginning of winter or the onset of spring.

In *The Book of Chuang Tzu*, a Taoist master is ill and close to death. He tells his grieving family and friend:

> The cosmos gives me form, brings me
> to birth,

guides me into old age and settles
me in death.

If I think my life good, then I must
think my death good.

Finally the master says, "Peacefully we die,
calmly we awake."[2]

We must respect our cats in their old age,
and, when the time comes, help them to die
peacefully so they may awake calmly.

Your cat's death may come naturally. He may
simply fall asleep and not wake again in this lifetime.

Although that is a good way to pass from this
life, it is not the only peaceful death a cat can
experience. If your cat is very sick or in extreme
pain, it is a kindness to your friend to help him
leave this world. Euthanasia by painless injec-
tion can be a gentle gift.

Listen to your cat as he faces the end of his
life. Let him tell you when it is time to go. Many
terminally ill cats will tell you they are ready to
let go by refusing food and water.

My Silver Lining had suffered from progressively worse arthritis during her final year. Then one day she suddenly started dragging her back legs; she couldn't walk. I took her immediately into the veterinarian's office. We spent the afternoon taking X rays and other tests to determine whether she had a problem that could be resolved.

I didn't hear the diagnosis from the veterinarian until the next morning. But Silver Lining gave me the verdict that night. For fifteen years my big gray cat had chosen to sleep at the foot of my bed. That evening she crawled up into my arms and stayed there the entire night. She purred and sang to me and said good-bye.

The next morning my veterinarian said that Silver Lining had ruptured a disk. Given her arthritic condition, other significant health problems, and her age, no treatment would provide a good quality of life for my old girl.

Silver Lining was calm and unafraid as I held her and had her gently put to sleep. She was

ready to let go of life that had been held by a
slender thread for several months.

Although I will always miss her, I feel content
that she passed away when she was ready to let
go. During her last few months she had illnesses
that made me wonder if she was ready to let go,
but she struggled to get better. With her final
episode there was no struggle, just peace.

Practical Application of the Tao: Dealing with Grief

The Book of Chuang Tzu describes a friend coming over to console Chuang Tzu after the great
sage's wife died. The friend was startled to see
Chuang Tzu pounding a battered tub and sing-
ing. When his friend told Chuang Tzu that his
actions were not right, the great master replied,

When she first died, I certainly mourned
just like everyone else! However, I then
thought back to her birth and to the very

roots of her being, before she was born. Indeed, not just before she was born but before the time when her body was created. Not just before her body was created but before the very origin of her life's breath. Out of all this, through the wonderful mystery of change she was given her life's breath. Her life's breath wrought a transformation and she had a body. Her body wrought a transformation and she was born. Now there is yet another transformation and she is dead. She is like the four seasons in the way that spring, summer, autumn and winter follow each other. She is now at peace, lying in her chamber, but if I were to sob and cry it would certainly appear that I could not comprehend the ways of destiny. This is why I stopped.[3]

Even Chuang Tzu mourned his loss for a period of time. We honor our cats by grieving for them. They loved us and we loved them. It is right to grieve. But at some point it is time to let

that grief go. That is also a part of our relationship with the life of our cat.

If this stage of our being can be wondrous, so
can the next. Release the spirit of your cat to
allow him to transition joyfully back to the Tao.

PART FIVE

Living
in the
Tao

15

WISE SOULS

How much more lonely and barren human existence would be if an ancient cat and an ancient person had not found each other. This loving, joyful, social creature each day gives us her trust and friendship. We are just beginning to learn how to return that love.

When I was working on this book, I asked many people why cats always sit right next to people with cat allergies and other "noncat" people. One person answered, "It is because the cat is sure that if the person just gets to know him better, the person will like him. So the cat sits there, waiting for the person to understand what a good creature he really is."

Collectively, cats are waiting on humankind. It is time to treat the cat not as a deity and not as a devil but as an equal. She is a creature who deserves respect, admiration, and care.

We have much to learn from our animal companions. By following the lessons our cats have to teach us, we can come closer to the natural, pure path that we were meant to follow. Through the lives of our cats, we catch a glimpse of the Tao.

Every cat has countless lessons for humankind to learn. These are a few that have occurred to me.

External Circumstances

Over the millennia, humans have treated cats as sacred beings. In Egypt Bastet (the goddess of music, dance, and revelry) was portrayed as a woman with a cat's head or as a giant cat. In ancient Egypt killing a cat was punishable by death.

Birman cats may have been sacred in some Buddhist temples. Cat deities were given credit for crop fertility in China and Ireland. No other domestic animal has ever received such widespread adulation.

Sadly, no other domestic animal has received

such widespread persecution. Cats have been linked with witchcraft and been tortured. In 1484 Pope Innocent VIII ordered all cats killed. Millions were burned to death. Even to this day, thrill-seeking sociopaths are far more likely to torture and kill cats than any other animal.

Throughout this turbulent history of adoration and abuse, cats have remained unaffected. They are the same, whether being exalted or excoriated.

We can adopt the dignity of our cats. Whether we have just been awarded a big promotion or are unemployed, whether we live in a mansion or a shack: These are external circumstances. They should not affect our hearts.

Chuang Tzu wrote:

Life and death, profit and loss, failure and success, poverty and wealth, value and worthlessness, praise and blame, hunger and thirst, cold and heat — these are natural changes in the order of things. They alternate with one another like day and night.

No one knows where one ends and the other begins. Therefore, they should not disturb our peace or enter into our souls. Live so that you are at ease, in harmony with the world, and full of joy. Day and night, share the springtime with all things, thus creating the seasons in your own heart. This is called achieving full harmony.[1]

A cat carries himself with his own dignity. He accepts or rejects contact with another creature based on what he chooses to do. You cannot convince a cat to do something he does not want to do. He is internally motivated. We can choose to be more like our cats.

By following our cats' example, we can live in harmony with the world, full of joy.

Sleep

Cats average about eighteen hours of sleep a day. Cats don't feel guilty for taking time to sleep. They don't keep themselves awake, trying to complete an extra task. When they are tired, they sleep.

Human body rhythms are different from cats', but the lesson remains the same. When we are tired, we should sleep.

Focus

A cat can sit and wait at a mouse hole for hours. An indoor cat will stare at an insect on the wall for twenty minutes. The cat will process and dismiss extraneous noises with a flick of one ear. When the cat is focused, nothing can distract her mind.

Patience

A cat can be endlessly patient. She will plan for hours, even days, how to catch a bird or tease the dog. She does not seek instant solutions. Instead, she waits, she sleeps, she dreams, and then she pounces.

The Inner Eye

Humans evaluate other people by their appearance or their social status. We even judge animals by the superficial standards that we call beauty.

Cats do not care about exterior appearances. They are not fooled by people who pretend to be kind. A person must be honest, or a cat will not respond. Cats do care about whether or not the other creature is safe and trustworthy.

Lao Tzu wrote:

> The five colors
> blind our eyes.
> The five notes
> deafen our ears.
> The five flavors
> dull our taste.

He concludes:

So the wise soul
watches with the inner
not the outward eye,
letting that go,
keeping this.[2]

We can learn to be more like our cats. We can look past exterior pretenses and judge people by the kindness, character, and honesty they exhibit.

The Sixth Sense

Cats tell you when a storm or an earthquake is coming. Many cats have been lost hundreds of miles away from their houses and found their way home. More amazingly, there have been documented cases in which cats have traveled hundreds of miles to find the new home where their human household members have moved.

Cats are so internally silent that they can hear

the footfall of a mouse a dozen yards away. They feel the flickering wings of a butterfly in the neighbor's yard. Certainly they can sense the qi of the people they love.

A true Taoist master understands his subject so well that he becomes a part of it. In that sense, cats are masters of the universe.

Let your cat show you how to be still. Learn from her how to relax and regain the rhythm of the earth and sky down to the depths of your existence.

Quiet Voices

Cats are the quietest of creatures, yet they are extraordinarily capable of getting what they need. A silent stare at an empty food bowl almost always produces results. Your quiet friend will gently lie down on your book, making it clear that it is time to pay attention. A well-timed rub against an ankle or a purr will almost always be met with a caress from a human.

Cats show us how much we can accomplish without shouting and screaming. We can achieve more with gentle persistence than constant attack.

Claws are reserved for serious threats.

Healers

If you live with a cat, it is almost a pleasure to be sick in bed. There is exquisite comfort in feeling your cat curl up next to you. She provides you with the warmth of her body. She may bathe your fevered skin with her tongue. She gives to you the healing magic of her purr.

Cats are effective healers. Stroking a cat has tangible medical benefits for humans, lowering our blood pressure and reducing the pain of arthritis. People heal more quickly from major illness when they are in the healing presence of cats.

When our human or animal friends are ill, we

can choose to share our own hearts just as fully and generously as our cats share theirs.

Sages

It is a human trait to search constantly for the sages, the shamans, of our world. I know people who have traveled around the globe just for the chance to be in the presence of wise souls. Those quests may be valuable for those who take them, but we do not have to go on a pilgrimage to find a sage.

Because cats are so common, so ordinary, it is easy to forget how uncommon and extraordinary they really are. They are gentle teachers and loving friends. Their purrs resonate with the primal rhythm of the universe. They are seers and healers.

By letting down the walls we humans have manufactured between ourselves and these small, wise souls, we can become better, happier, and more patient. Through them, we can feel what it is like to fly like the birds and pounce like a tiger. We learn how to play again. We remember the best parts of ourselves.

I do not have to take a journey to find a shaman. I have a sage sitting on my windowsill.

WORKS CITED

Chapter 1
1. Gia-Fu Feng and Jane English, *Lao Tsu: Tao Te Ching* (New York: Vintage Books, 1972), Chapter 1.

Chapter 2
1. Ursula K. Le Guin, *Lao Tzu Tao Te Ching: A Book About the Way and the Power of the Way* (Boston: Shambala Publications, 1997), p. 37 (Chapter 27).
2. Martin Palmer with Elizabeth Breuilly, *The Book of Chuang Tzu* (London: Arkana, 1996), p. 50.

Chapter 3
1. Martin Palmer with Elizabeth Breuilly, *The Book of Chuang Tzu* (London: Arkana, 1996), p. 180.

Chapter 5
1. Martin Palmer with Elizabeth Breuilly, *The Book of Chuang Tzu* (London: Arkana, 1996), pp. 32–33.
2. Feng and English, *Lao Tsu: Tao Te Ching*, Chapter 63.

Chapter 8
1. Le Guin, *Lao Tzu Tao Te Ching: A Book About the Way and the Power of the Way*, p. 35 (Chapter 25).

Chapter 9
1. Gai-Fu Feng and Jane English, *Lao Tsu: Tao Te Ching* (New York: Vintage Books, 1972), Chapter 78.
2. Martin Palmer with Elizabeth Breuilly, *The Book of Chuang Tzu* (London: Arkana, 1996), p. 188.
3. Ibid., pp. 106–107.

Chapter 10

1. Gia-Fu Feng and Jane English, *Lao Tsu: Tao Te Ching* (New York: Vintage Books, 1972), Chapter 30.

Chapter 12

1. Martin Palmer with Elizabeth Breuilly, *The Book of Chuang Tzu* (London: Arkana, 1996), p. 67.
2. Robert G. Hendricks, *Lao-Tzu: Te-Tao Ching* (New York: Ballantine Books, 1989), p. 81 (Chapter 29).

Chapter 14

1. Gia-Fu Feng and Jane English, *Lao Tsu: Tao Te Ching* (New York: Vintage Books, 1972), Chapter 33.
2. Martin Palmer with Elizabeth Breuilly, *The Book of Chuang Tzu* (London: Arkana, 1996), p. 54.
3. Ibid., p. 151.

Chapter 15

1. Gia-Fu Feng and Jane English, *Chuang Tsu: Inner Chapters* (New York: Vintage Books, 1974), p. 105.
2. Ursula K. Le Guin, *Lao Tzu Tao Te Ching: A Book About the Way and the Power of the Way* (Boston: Shambala Publications, 1997), p. 15 (Chapter 12).

DEBORAH WOOD is a pet columnist for *The Oregonian,* writing articles on dogs, cats, and other domesticated animals. She is a veteran dog trainer and uses only nonviolent Taoist methods of training. She competes in obedience trials with her papillon dogs. Deborah Wood is also the author of *The Tao of Bow Wow.*

Printed in the United States
by Baker & Taylor Publisher Services